GOODNESS AND MERCY

God bless your family
as He has mine!

Esther Davison

GOODNESS AND MERCY

Esther Davison

ISBN - 978-1-936107-25-4
ISBN - 1-936107-25-2
LCCN - 2009936592

Cover Design by Alan Pranke
Typeset by Peggy LeTrent
Second printing 2015
Printed in the United States of America

INTRODUCTION

The impetus for writing this book came from my daughter when, on a long road trip from Wyoming to Michigan, we listened to six audio tapes made by my mother about her experiences in China. We laughed and cried all the way across Nebraska, Iowa and Michigan as we listened to her story. Jennifer, my daughter, had not known the whole story before and insisted that I write it down. "People will come to trust in God because of her story," she said.

Without the help and encouragement of my family, I would not have completed this story. My sisters both sent me material they had accumulated and my husband read and edited the last version. My daughter-in-law, Aimee, drew the maps, something I could never do. Friends I taught school with kept urging me (really "nagging" would be a better word) to complete it. Friends in my church encouraged me.

Maybeth's story is not complete. The ways that God has provided for my family are merely begun here. More than anything else, the proof of God's care for his children has driven me to complete this part of the story. My reason for writing it can best be summed up in a Scripture my mother used to quote regularly: "And thou shalt remember all the way which the LORD thy God led thee these forty years in the wilderness." She was convinced that we must remind our children of God's faithfulness, goodness, and mercy in hard times, so that we will have strength for the times ahead in our lives.

1

PROLOGUE

A junk was approaching fast behind them on the river. Night was falling, and as they watched the approaching junk, a shout rang out from a shadowy figure standing in the bow. He demanded that they surrender to him. Since he had a crew of six men and Charles Judd had only his friend, the boatman, they quickly raised their hands and bowed their heads in an attitude of surrender. Pulling along side, a dark figure with menacing eyes jumped into their small boat. Holding his long sword above his head, he made them kneel in the bottom of the boat while he snarled that he was going to take them back to the nearest village and hand them over to the headman.

Hunan province in 1877 was an area of China hostile to "foreign devils," as any white man was called. Charles and his Chinese boatman had traveled for two thousand miles in almost three months along the Yangtze and Yuan rivers and had met with much hardship, but also many friendly and interested Chinese. Charles was dressed in Chinese clothing and from the back of his shaved head a long pigtail, or queue, extended down his back in the style worn in the last imperial dynasty of China. He and his friend had been telling the Chinese the story of a man named Jesus, who was the Son of God, and had died so that their sins could be forgiven.

Officially, they had passports and permission to travel in inland China, but each village was a government unto itself. Many of the villages they had passed through on their journey were cruelly oppressed by opium lords who held themselves above the central government and harbored intense hatred toward foreigners.

Sitting close to Charles in the boat as the junk towed them back toward the nearest village on the river, the pirate gingerly tested the edge of his long sword with his thumb. Several of his crew sat in the bow with swords strapped to their belts and guns in their hands. Charles and his friend sat in silence and an attitude of meekness.

When their credentials were given to the local opium lord, he said, "I do not want these. Seize his boat."

Charles' friend translated a quick chatter of conversation among the pirates. "They intend to hold us until dark and then kill us and rob us," he said. Five hours of threatening flourishes with swords and guns being shot close over their heads ensued until, according to Charles Judd, there looked to be "little human hope of escape."

Praying that God would work a miracle while trying to strengthen his boatman's faith, Charles Judd waited for nightfall. As the dark began to close in, the pirate went back to his junk for a meal leaving only one crewman on Judd's boat. The light had gone and the night was completely dark. Suddenly, out of the nothingness, a third boat came crashing into the side of Judd's boat. The pirates jumped to attention and much confusion ensued. In the melee, Judd loosed the moorings of his little boat and grabbing the oars rowed away as fast as he could down river. The pirate crewman, seeing he was outnumbered, jumped over the side and swam back upriver to his companions.

Escape from the pirates was only the beginning of their night. The river was a dangerous place to travel in the daytime when one could see steep drop-offs and rapids approaching. For an hour Judd rowed as hard as he could, his muscles quivering with fatigue. He had covered twenty miles before he eased up on his furious pace. No rapids slowed his forward progress and, in the dark the pirates gave up the chase.

God had answered his prayers and delivered him from danger once more in this foreign land.

PART ONE - PREPARATION FOR SERVICE

"How firm a foundation, ye saints of the Lord
Is laid for your faith in His excellent Word.
What more can He say than to you He hath said?
To you who for refuge to Jesus have fled."

CHAPTER ONE

Maybeth Judd walked up the gangplank with a straight back, head up and chin slightly forward. It was September 1936, and she was one of twenty girls, leaving Vancouver, headed for China. She was tall, probably 5'8" at least, thin, with masses of dark brown hair pulled back into a low bun and gentle waves framing her face. Her prominent nose contrasted with deep-set green eyes. Hundreds of people waved from the dock below and streamers ran up to the deck of the ship, fluttering bravely in the breeze. Far below she could see her parents looking very small and far away. She was twenty-three and planned to serve God as a missionary.

It hadn't always been her plan. In fact, the idea of being a missionary anywhere was the last thing she had planned for herself. But she felt compelled to go, compelled, not by parents or peers, but by God Himself. Although she appeared as confident as any passenger that day, she hid nagging fears as she anticipated the trip to far away China. China was in the throes of a civil war with Nationalist forces struggling for supremacy against a growing Communist threat. In addition, war with Japan was imminent. Cruel warlords ruled many provinces, fighting vicious wars with neighboring warlords. In a country lacking strong centralized government, bandits roamed the countryside, stealing from houses and killing travelers. The country was, at best, unstable.

The lump in her throat wouldn't go away. She feared being away from her parents and the accompanying homesickness. She already dreaded the familiar seasickness she knew would plague her for the entire trip. Outwardly shy by nature, she hardly looked like an adventurer to distant lands, but a spirit of determination filled her as she set her face for China. Little did she know the adventure that lay before her! War was about to break out and she would spend most of the next 9 years with little peace, living the life of a refugee. But Maybeth was focused and ready; always a person of action, once she set her mind to a task, she welcomed action and was eager to get started.

Missionary work was not new to her. Her grandparents had been missionaries in China, serving their God under the often hostile eye of imperial dynasties in remote areas of China, a part of Asia, which was, at that time, no more civilized than a medieval feudal society. Her grandfather, Charles Judd, had traveled up the Yangtze in the latter years of the 19th century and preached in areas of China closed to foreigners and suspicious of outside influence. Her father, Charles Judd, Jr., had served God in the China of treaty ports and opium trade. Missionary work in China was in her blood and it was no surprise to her family that she was going back to the China she had known as a child.

Maybeth was sponsored by the same missionary society that her parents had served with, a missionary society well respected by both the Chinese and the rest of the world. It was the China Inland Mission, founded in the late 1800's by a British visionary, J. Hudson Taylor.

This was not the first such missionary society serving in China. But it was the first one to emphasize working in unreached areas of China, areas that had not been exposed to the white man and his God. It emphasized social equality with the Chinese not found in other societies of the day. China Inland Mission missionaries dressed like the Chinese, lived as much as possible in typical Chinese homes, and had shed the " white man's burden" attitude of a majority of foreigners with influence in Asia. Maybeth's father, Charles, had grown a long pigtail, of which he was very proud, also called a queue, part of the dress code for a scholar in imperial China, and her parents had been married in Chinese wedding clothes.

Another striking difference in the China Inland Mission, or the CIM as it was called, was its emphasis on faith. Hudson Taylor, the mission founder, had said, "God's work done in God's way will never lack God's supply." CIM missionaries did not ask anyone for support. They did not go into homeland churches to raise the support they would need for a

8

term. They simply applied to the CIM and, if accepted, trusted God for the means.

And God did supply their needs. Remarkable stories of the provision of God had been related to Maybeth by her parents and grandparents. The mission society had survived without pleas for support for almost fifty years now. She believed that God would care for her and only bring into her life those experiences that were for her good and for His glory. So, pushing her fears away, her spirit was confident as she boarded the ship that would take her back to a familiar place. Yet that familiar place was a very different place and time, and China was an unpredictable and volatile place in the fall of 1936.

Only parts of China were familiar to Maybeth. Her parents had worked in Shanghai and Maybeth and her older sister Kathy had spent long winter vacations from boarding school bicycling around the streets of Shanghai. Sometimes the two sisters and their father would get up early in the morning and ride out of the city into the surrounding countryside, stopping for breakfast at a roadside stand. There they would enjoy a steaming bowl of noodles or a hot sweet potato. Those were times that were very precious to Maybeth, her sister Kathy, and her father, Charles Judd.

The other part of China that was familiar to her was the beach community of Chefoo (Yantai) in Shantung (Shandong) province. Chefoo was the location of the boarding school Maybeth attended when she turned six years old and where she remained as a student until she was sixteen, nearly through high school.

Chefoo, as the school itself came to be called, was the boarding school that all the children of missionaries with the China Inland Mission attended. Maybeth was a second generation Chefooite; her father also attended Chefoo, as did many of the children of early missionaries in China. In fact, the boarding school had been founded by Hudson Taylor for the benefit of the six Judd boys, Maybeth's father and his brothers. The boarding school, from its founding days onward, had earned a place of high regard among Europeans in China. Its association with Oxford and use of the Oxford examinations made it a reputable school for the children of business personnel of British companies in China as well as the CIM missionaries' children.

Maybeth had many memories of her days in Chefoo. She had not always been a compliant child and had in fact heard from missionary friends years after she left, that she was often the subject of prayer because of her wild and rebellious ways. Maybeth loved a good adventure. One night she persuaded a group of girls to climb out the third story windows of their dormitory and walk around the building on a six-inch ledge, risking certain death if they were to fall to the asphalt courtyard below. On one of several such occasions, the girls, in their white nighties were lined up on the ledge, barefoot with small hands and feet clinging to the rough stone of the building. The elderly Chinese night watchman appeared in the courtyard below, and the girls feared the worst.

Certain that they would be expelled and sent back to their parents in disgrace, they froze, and, after he had left, crept back to their bedroom windows, climbed in, stood in a circle, held hands, and vowed never to do something that foolish again. It was simple good fortune, or the providence of God that they were not reported. The old night watchman, seeing the fluttering white nightgowns, thought that perhaps he had seen spirits and was too frightened to tell anyone. Maybeth had plenty of spunk even if sometimes it was tinged with a certain daredevil attitude.

One night at a beach meeting there on the coast of China, God spoke to her personally. A special series of meetings for the children in the boarding school featured a special speaker. Webb-Peploe, a missionary from India, quickly won the hearts of the children with his warmth and genuineness. He preached on the 53rd chapter from the Old Testament prophet, Isaiah. The prophet Isaiah wrote of the coming Messiah who would die for the sins of the world. It was a moment Maybeth would remember for the rest of her life. The missionary urged the students to, "Put your name in verse 3. 'He was wounded for our transgressions. He was bruised for our iniquity. With His stripes we are healed.'"

When Maybeth, with eyes opened by the Spirit of God, did as Webb-Peploe asked, the Scripture read: "He was wounded for Maybeth's transgressions; he was bruised for Maybeth's iniquity; and with his stripes, Maybeth is healed." It struck her that Christ had suffered for her sins, both remembered and forgotten. She realized that it was for her that He had died and she eagerly received Christ's righteousness for herself. Kneeling there on the sand and putting her name into that verse, this child of God was brought into a personal relationship with Jesus Christ.

Looking back on it now, she knew that it was then that her life really changed. She started to live not for herself, but for God, in a genuine way. God had changed her focus.

CHAPTER TWO

Now here she was with nineteen other young lady missionaries headed for China. The ship was one of a Japanese line and a stopover in Japan was a special treat offered by the shipping company.

*Maybeth (third from right) and friends pose
on board ship on their way to Japan.*

Maybeth suffered the expected seasickness, as her previous experience on ships had taught her. She was miserably sick from the first gentle motion of the ship away from the dock until she stood on firm land again. Fresh air sometimes helped, but overall the weeks of sea travel were a nightmare.

Photographs in a small album Maybeth made during her first year in China show several pictures of the trip and one in particular of the sea, stretching away to the horizon, with the notation beneath, "Ten days without seeing land!" But printed above the picture are the words of a children's chorus, "Wide, wide, as the ocean.../ High as the heavens above.../ Deep, deep as the deepest sea,/ Is my Savior's love. / I, though so unworthy,/ Still am a child of His care,/ For His word teaches me,/ That His love reaches me,/ Everywhere." Seasickness notwithstanding, Maybeth knew that His love supported her.

As soon as the ship docked in Tokyo, the seasickness subsided, and true to its word the shipping company treated the girls royally. They were taken to Mt. Fuji and to tea in a Japanese garden in Nagasaki, a city that would be decimated by the coming war. In fact, while Maybeth was being treated as a special guest, the Japanese were massing troops in Manchuria and would soon invade China. The invasion of Manchuria in 1932 had been sanctioned by the emperor after seeing the easy success of unsanctioned attacks by the Japanese armies. Soon, thousands of Japanese civilians were swarming to new land in Manchuria and the Japanese-supported puppet government brutalized the indigenous population.

Manchurian guerilla resistance on at least one occasion resulted in a Japanese train derailment and in revenge thousands of soldiers were set loose upon the countryside, burning, looting, killing indiscriminately and assaulting young girls, some as young as ten years old. Contests were reported between Japanese soldiers to determine who could kill 250 Manchurians or Chinese first. Generally the most ferocious and xenophobic soldiers were chosen by Japanese generals to carry out work in the countryside.

Oblivious to the mayhem in Manchuria, as most of the world was, the young women boarded ship again and sailed south to Shanghai. The city was as she remembered it as a child, the harbor at the Bund, the embankment along the riverfront in Shanghai, crowded with tiny houseboats and merchants selling food and trinkets. Towering over the harbor were the many storied European buildings, their architecture strangely dissonant with the surrounding squalor.

Shanghai harbor and the buildings of the European concession, known as "the Bund," in 1936.

Enroute from the harbor to the CIM compound on Sinza road, the taxi weaved its way through busy streets where traffic was directed by Indian men in turbans. Many businessmen wore European style tailored suits though some still wore the traditional long silk gown. Women of the upper class were dressed in brightly colored silk with elaborate embroidery while those of the working class wore short jackets and trousers. Rickshaws streaked through every space in the traffic pattern and cars and trucks swept through the streets while pedestrians dashed for safety. English signs with incorrect English usage adorned shops with messages like "We give fits upstairs," on a tailor's shop. The young women were transfixed with the sights and constantly speeding traffic. Such a modern city was not the picture of China they had imagined.

When the taxi turned off the main thoroughfares, though, Maybeth and her friends saw plenty of the other side of Shanghai. Beggars and dirty streets turned the picture black and white, a world that contrasted with the brightly colored silks and signs of the main streets.

The China Inland Mission compound in the foreign concession occupied some ten acres in Shanghai. Arriving there was almost like coming home. Maybeth discovered some of the secretaries there who had known her father and she remembered parts of the city from bicycle trips she had enjoyed as a child. Many fond childhood memories of Shanghai flooded her thoughts. The Mission complex was in a different area of the city now, a very delightful area of the foreign concession. The Mission headquarters consisted of several large three-story buildings with huge meeting rooms and comfortable suites. Its third floor was a hospital with much of the modern technology of the day available.

Following the First Opium War in 1842, many cities were opened up to trade with foreign countries. Areas of the treaty ports allowing extraordinary foreign home rule had been given to the countries doing trade with China and those areas were under the rule of the foreign government owning the concession. In 1936 the foreign concessions were like a little bit of home in the middle of Shanghai. Huge European style buildings and shops dominated the skyline and English was spoken everywhere. The young women felt as though they had landed in part of London. English-speaking-only clubs and businesses flocked to the lucrative trade in these concessions. In fact, in many areas of Shanghai, any Chinese businessman who did not speak some form of English was ignored or even mistreated.

Within a week the new recruits were sent upriver to language school. Language school took place in Yangchow, (Yangzhou) 150 miles up the Yangtze River from Shanghai. The school occupied a massive Romanesque style building with a huge veranda supported by rounded arches.

Huge European style buildings often characterized the buildings of mission-ary societies. This impressive building housed the women's language school.

It was easily large enough to accommodate nineteen young women and some of their teachers. Large sitting rooms and dining rooms were furnished in European style and tea was served every day in the late afternoon. The teachers, however, were Chinese and soon the women were introduced to a six month long saturation course in the Chinese language. They endured daily instruction in groups and individually. Although Maybeth had been born and raised in China, her grasp of the language was not particularly good since she had spent most of each year since she was six in boarding school.

It was hard work, but a good time to become acclimated to Chinese language and culture. Maybeth, in particular, in the tradition of her parents, wanted to live like the Chinese and dress like the Chinese so her days in language school caused her some anguish. She found the study

17

difficult, and she longed to be out among the people sharing the Gospel. In time, she was outfitted in long padded Chinese gowns with high stand-up collars and many buttons all the way down the side fastened to little loops. Pictures in her photo album showed Maybeth and her friends attempting the use of chopsticks and buttoning up all the buttons on those long cotton gowns.

Yangchow was a different world to Maybeth. She found the poverty and filthiness greater than she could have imagined. Her childhood experiences in China had been filled with bicycle riding through European style streets and eating hot Chinese dumplings bought from roadside stands.

Somehow her child eyes had not noticed the dreadful shabbiness and poverty of Chinese cities. Yangchow was on the Grand Canal and the houses were packed next to the canal with streets so narrow two couldn't walk abreast in them. Houses were made out of mud brick with thatched roofs. Often the household's animals scuttled through the family living quarters and fought for scraps beside children in paper-thin clothing.

Men and women could be seen walking the narrow streets with a bucket of water hanging from each end of a shoulder pole, the day's supply collected from the river or the canal. There was no public transportation and the people of the city generally were born, lived their lives, and died in the city, walking everywhere they needed to go. Some who had fields in the country would walk up to ten miles each way in a day, preferring to live in the city and return each night to the relative safety of the walls and closed gates. Everything was carried on the shoulder pole or by water buffalo if one could afford it. Rickshaws and wheelbarrow carts, pulled by coolies, carried those who could afford to pay.

The canal was the supply of water for drinking and cooking. It also was the sewer and the main mode of transportation. Disease and death stalked those who lived in such circumstances. Dysentery killed those too weak to fight it off. Tuberculosis was common and life expectancy was little more than 30 or 40 years.

Houseboats crowd the banks of the canals in Yangzhou. Many families had no other home and lived for generations on a houseboat.

Beggars were everywhere; most had no hope for any sort of life outside of begging. Some were lame and some simply poor. The sick and dying often begged in the streets and the typical family felt well off if they ate meat once a week. Most meals consisted of noodles and perhaps a few vegetables raised in the garden plot behind the house.

Peasants worked small plots of land, often no more then four or five acres, outside the city walls and were forced to pay large sums, in either produce or currency, for taxes to the local, often unscrupulous, administrators. Sometimes terrible debt was incurred and moneylenders, often the tax collectors themselves, charged up to 40% interest. Families in debt would sometimes have to sell children to pay their debts. Bandits roamed the countryside, relatively uncontrolled, and those who could not fight them chose to live in the walled city where there was some protection.

Maybeth's eyes were opened to the grinding poverty of the typical Chinese family as she observed city life as an adult. She longed to tell these people of the hope of heaven and of the love of God so that their burden there in Yangchow could be eased. In her halting Chinese she did speak to many and received mostly polite nods and smiles in return.

Sometimes in the evenings, as she sat down at the end of a hard day of study, Maybeth would wonder if she would ever marry. She longed to be married and raise a family, but she saw no way she would share the burden of the work with a husband. Although she put it out of her mind, she anticipated living her years in China in celibacy. The ship that had brought them to Shanghai had had twenty ladies on it. The boat behind had 5 single men. That proportion was typical of missionaries in China. In later years she would say with a wry smile that in church appeals for missionaries, many young men would volunteer saying, " Here am I; send my sister."

She knew that single missionary women often led very lonely lives. They were assigned to work in the CIM with other single ladies and sometimes the matches were difficult. It was another matter of trust in the God who had sent her there; that whatever came into her life was of God and would be welcomed.

Maybeth had been strongly influenced by the writings of Amy Carmichael, a pioneer missionary to India. Miss Carmichael's message of the disciplined life, a life that modeled a disciple of Christ, continually spoke to her. If she was going to be a disciple, how could she expect a life easier than the one the Master had led? Why should she expect a beautiful home and loving family when He had not found those things on earth? She was committed to lead a life of service to God and she would trust Him to take care of her needs. An often-quoted poem written by Amy Carmichael moved her to greater trust:

Make me Thy Fuel
From prayer that asks that I may be
Sheltered from winds that beat on Thee

From fearing when I should aspire
From faltering when I should climb higher

From silken self, O Captain,
Free Thy soldier who would follow Thee

From subtle love of softening things
From easy choices, weakenings

Not thus are spirits fortified
Not this way went the Crucified.

From all that dims Thy Calvary
O Lamb of God, deliver me

Give me the love that leads the way
The faith that nothing can dismay

The hope no disappointments tire
The passion that will burn like fire

Let me not sink to be a clod
Make me Thy fuel, Flame of God.   Amy Carmichael

CHAPTER THREE

As the end of language school approached and the time came to assign Mission stations, all the young women in the language school were anxious. Coming from America and Canada, a number from Australia, and a majority from England, they had formed a close friendship in those six months. They knew that they would be scattered across China, with other missionaries to learn the work. During those months they prayed very much that God would guide the leaders of the CIM in their decisions of assignment for each of them as new workers.

A pioneer missionary was the picture Maybeth had drawn for herself, somewhere in Mongolia or Tibet, standing on a pile of stones, and preaching the gospel to people who had perhaps never seen a white woman. She scorned the dangers and looked forward with eagerness to an adventure-filled life. Confident she was going to be a real pioneer, she prayed with this plan in mind. "Somewhere along the Burmese border would be fine," she assured the Lord. She certainly did not want to be anywhere near the coast where missionaries worked in long-established churches. She wanted to work for God somewhere new and fascinating.

The day to assign stations arrived. Mr. Warren, a soft-spoken old man, deputy director of the CIM, with a long white beard and saintly air, interviewed Maybeth and said, "Now, Maybeth, we have been praying about your designation and looking into your past and your capabilities, and we've decided to put you into a Bible teaching ministry among women in a church that is already established up the coast of China from Yangchow where you are now."

"Oh no," Maybeth thought with a sinking heart, "Who wants to go to such a nearby place? I want to really travel. I want to do some real pioneer work. I want challenge and danger." But she said none of those things to Dr. Warren.

Instead, she obediently agreed to go up the coast of China to an established work; she was disappointed. Why would she be assigned to something as ordinary as a teaching work near the coast? She had such a desire to serve God in remote and hard places. She was ready to suffer hardship or even die for her Lord, and yet she had been denied that chance, she thought.

After a good cry in her room, she was reminded of the training of her youth, and, searching for answers, she turned to the Scriptures. As she read, one verse struck her. It was in Romans 12, verse 2, "The will of the Lord is good, acceptable, and perfect." God's will is always perfect, she realized, and she had prayed that God's will be made clear to the leaders of the Mission who designated her. She had prayed, "Lord, I know where I want to go, but let the men who designate me know where I should go according to Your will." So she trusted God and knew that it would indeed be good, and acceptable, and perfect.

What Maybeth did not know was that the area she was assigned was to be right in the middle of the coming war and nowhere in the remote western regions would she be tested as she would be in this eastern part of China. God did know her, and He would test her there on the coast.

The Olympic Games in Berlin in 1936 had displayed the beginnings of the racist policies that would characterize Germany in much of Europe in the years to come. Hitler was in control and his eyes were reaching far beyond the borders of Germany. The world began to brace for another war though few understood how devastating that war would be. Now, in 1937, in the Far East another imperialistic power was occupying North China. The Chinese government, in the spirit of appeasement, had, in essence, ceded most of North China to a puppet government run by the Japanese. War with Japan was inevitable.

CHAPTER FOUR

In late spring 1937, Maybeth traveled north by canal to an area of China near the coast. The area she had viewed as too tame for her adventurous spirit would prove to be far more dangerous than her imagined assignment further inland. The year 1937 was to be a year of tumult in China. The Nationalist Army under the leadership of Chiang Kai-Shek was facing a two-pronged problem. For many years the greatest threat to the still young Nationalist government had been the Communist threat under the leadership of Mao Tse-tung. In 1933, only three years before Maybeth arrived in China, the Communists controlled a large part of eastern China centered mainly in the southern provinces. The church, and especially the missionaries, was often the target of Communist anger against foreign influence. Many Chinese churches in the southern provinces were destroyed under Communist/war lord rule and many Christians executed publicly as examples.

A reunification of the Nationalist Army to include several independent war lords under Chiang Kai-Shek eventually succeeded in pushing the Communist Army out of the East. In the ensuing weeks his army sent 120,000 Communist soldiers on what would later be called "the Long March" to the west and finally over rugged terrain and mountains to the northern province of Yenan. In that remote area, their leader, Mao, successfully held out against the Nationalists. There he set up his Communist headquarters and rebuilt his army.

With Mao in the far northwest, Chiang could ignore the problem for a while, but trouble between the Nationalist forces and the Communist forces continued throughout the war with Japan in spite of a later tenuous alliance.

The other problem facing the Nationalist government was the

steady advance of the Japanese from Manchuria, which they controlled, into northern China. In 1936 Japanese reinforcements were sent to the borders of five northern provinces of China, probably preparatory to an invasion. The Chinese protested the military buildup and at an anti-Japanese demonstration, two Japanese were killed, followed by further killings. Chiang Kai-Shek apologized.

The Japanese accepted his apology and suggested that they help Chiang against the Communists, an offer he quickly refused. To him, apparently, the Japanese were worse bedfellows than the Communists, who were at least Chinese for the most part. Meanwhile Chiang had reinforced his own forces to include an area previously controlled by a Communist sympathizing warlord in southern Canton. In August, the month before Maybeth Judd sailed for China, Chiang Kai-Shek entered Canton for the first time in 11 years. Now, in early spring of 1937, as Maybeth traveled north from Yangchow, the struggle continued between Nationalist government forces and the Communist rebels. A proposal was made that they join forces to fight the Japanese, but Chiang Kai-Shek refused such an idea fearing that Japan would see it as saber-rattling and he did not want to give Japan a reason to begin all out war with China.

Meanwhile, unafraid of the trouble in the northern provinces and feeling that it was a regional problem far away, Maybeth journeyed up the canal to the small village of Lienshui in the province of Kiangsu (Jiangsu) to work with another single lady, Agnes Harrison.

Maybeth's decision to come to China as a missionary had not been an easy one. She had determined early that although she was willing to serve God, she was certainly not willing to become a missionary. She reasoned that her family had suffered enough in China. Her parents had lost a child to meningitis in China and had suffered poverty and separation many times. Surely it was enough for God. She and her sister, Kathy, had been separated from her parents in boarding school because that was the only way to be educated in China. Determined to have her way in this matter, she had refused to consider the foreign mission field as a way for her to serve God.

One night at a meeting in the CIM headquarters in Vancouver,

Maybeth heard a missionary relate a familiar story in the Bible in II Kings chapter 7, a story of a group of lepers who lived outside an Israelite city under siege by the Assyrians. The lepers were the castoffs of society because of their disease and confined to an area outside the gates of the besieged city. They knew that the people in the city were starving to death and they too were hungry. They went to the tents of the enemy hoping to beg for food, and found to their amazement that the enemy had fled and left their gold, clothing, and food. After the lepers gorged themselves, dressed in all the finery they could find, and filled their pockets with gold, they stopped to realize that the people in the city were still starving, unaware that they had been delivered. "This is a day of good tidings; but we hold our peace," the lepers said. Ashamed, they left their newfound luxury and ease and went to the city to share the good news with the starving people in the besieged city.

The story and the Scripture moved Maybeth, but she was still very unwilling to go to the foreign mission field. At that meeting, she prayed reluctantly, "God, I don't want to be a missionary. You know I've done my share out there with my parents. I offer myself if You want me to go, but please close the door."

God had instead opened doors for Maybeth and after three years of Bible School and summers of mission work in Alberta, she applied to the CIM and was turned down because she was too young. She spent a year in England, living in the CIM mission home in London and taking a course in homeopathic medicine. She applied again, was accepted and here she was beginning work on her first mission station.

Agnes Harrison, only two years older than Maybeth, was a charming English girl, who had spent her first years working with a very old single lady missionary, very rigid about how Agnes should do almost everything. Agnes had found it quite difficult to fit in to the work and the ways of her senior missionary. She knew, though, that God had lessons to teach her in this relationship and was willing to learn humility. When the senior missionary went on furlough and then on to retirement, Maybeth was assigned to take her place and work in the Chinese church there with Agnes.

27

The day that Maybeth arrived in Lienshui, Agnes met her and took her to the tiny room she was to have and there on the desk was a verse printed out, "Comforted by the coming of Maybeth," a quotation from one of the Apostle Paul's letters when he said he was comforted by the coming of Timothy. They were both very young and inexperienced, but they were glad to work together.

CHAPTER FIVE

Lienshui, in 1937, was a walled city like most of the cities in China at the time. China, since the 1911 revolution, when a longsuffering people had thrown off the chains of the Manchu empire, had been a society in chaos. The old feudal society had changed little in the countryside and populations still crowded into walled cities, built by warlords to prevent attack by neighboring warlords. The warlords were not as prevalent since a republic, at least in name, had been established in 1911. However the gates of the city were closed at night to protect from bandits in the generally lawless rural areas nearby. In recent years the city of Lienshui had built a canal to join the Grand Canal that went south to Nanking. The new canal ran right beside the walls of the city.

Lienshui was not unlike what Maybeth had found in the much larger city of Yangchow with mud brick houses for the most part and thatched roofs with dirt floors. Most of the people were farmers and farmed outside the walls of the city in the daylight hours, returning before the gates of the city closed at night. A local magistrate acted as the government agent and collected taxes from the people in the area, sometimes doubling their tax burden and lining his own pockets. Most peasants were uneducated and did not understand the system.

The CIM house in the city was one of the largest and had wooden floors, which were a luxury most in the city only dreamed of. It was in considerable disrepair though; it lacked screens and had a leaky roof. A house without screens on the windows meant that malaria was a great danger and so Maybeth and Agnes both slept under mosquito nets, which hung above their tiny cots and tucked into the mattress underneath them when they slept.

The city was north of Yangchow and had been exposed to the Gospel

29

of Christ for many years. In fact, a generation or two before, Mrs. Howard Taylor (Hudson Taylor's daughter-in-law) had worked there. She was a very godly person but still in that city they told the joke about someone bringing her a bench to sit on that had no back on it.

The Chinese who remembered Mrs. Taylor told Maybeth that they knew the English word for this bench: - "Oh," she asked, "What is it called?"

"Mrs. Taylor taught us the English name for this bench. The name is 'agony'." The Chinese were very pleased with their English instruction and Mrs. Taylor gave Maybeth reason for a little chuckle many years later.

Lienshui had a long and fascinating history. It was once a normally idolatrous place: many different idols held positions of prominence in the homes, in the temples, in pagodas, just as in all cities in China. The city was right on the banks of the Yellow river, before the river had been diverted into the new canal, and this river was the water supply for the whole city. Years before her arrival an extensive drought dried up the river, causing unimaginable hardship for the people there.

Their desperation caused them to pray continually to their idols for rain. They prayed on and on and the idols didn't answer. There was no rain and the river continued to dry up more and more. As a last resort, the city fathers declared that the idols needed a tour of the town. Carefully they packed up their city idols, put them in sedan chairs, partially covered chairs carried high on two poles between two men, and carried them on their shoulders through the streets. They took them down to the dry riverbank, and showed them the parched earth. They thought, "Now they understand and see what desperate straits we are in, they'll send us rain." And they returned their idols to the temples again.

They prayed and prayed and still there was no rain. Finally, in a fit of anger, the people of the entire city banded together, took the idols out of the temples and out of their homes, carried them down to the dry riverbank and smashed them on the stones, leaving no idols at all in the city.

Immediately a strange phenomenon occurred. Many in the city believed that their family members became possessed by demons. Incidents of what appeared to be demon possession increased dramatically with all the typical symptoms. Maybeth did not know if this story was a true episode of demon possession and had no ready answers. Some believed that idols were the habitations of demons and when the idols were destroyed the demons looked for other hosts. She remembered the story in the Gospels that told of Jesus casting the demons out of a man, and the demons begging to be sent into a herd of swine. But she did not know what to make of the demon possession claimed by many in the city.

Lienshui was still experiencing this phenomenon, as it never had before the destruction of its idols. Maybeth and Agnes Harrison, her co-worker, and the old Chinese pastor of the church dealt with many cases of what the relatives believed to be demon possession. Individuals brought to the church were exactly like the cases she had read about in the New Testament. Some arrived, tied to stretchers, screaming and foaming at the mouth. Sometimes they were saying, "There's three of us; there's three of us." At other times Maybeth and Agnes could hardly make out what they were saying. Strange and frightening noises erupted from inside them. The presence of evil was palpable.

These afflicted individuals were always taken to the old Chinese pastor, Mr. Chu. Agnes and Maybeth only watched. He would take the afflicted people to a room at the back of the church and talk with them. Then he would pray for them and with them, using the name of the Lord Jesus Christ, and many times they would come out of that back room walking calmly and speaking normally. Maybeth had no logical explanation for it, but simply observed this phenomenon whenever it took place and thanked God for the peace afforded the sufferers. She grew to love the old Chinese pastor, Chu, and was willing to trust him and accept his work among these troubled people.

Maybeth and Agnes helped with teaching the Bible to those who were thus changed and to the population in general, mostly illiterate peasants who had embraced Christianity for several generations.

Maybeth dutifully and perhaps because of some unconfessed homesickness, wrote letters home weekly to her parents in Vancouver. Even when the Japanese were threatening her life in later years, Maybeth's letters were always full of reassurance to her parents. She wrote of the work in the church, of the weather, of the presence of uninvited creatures in the house, and of the Christians' fervor for the singing of hymns.

The weather in that summer of 1937 was terribly hot and humid, since Kiangsu is a flat province close to the coast of China. The humidity was so great that when Maybeth took a pair of shoes out of a box to wear them, she found that they were covered with mold. But, nothing deterred, and with a typical buoyant spirit, she wrote her father that "the mold comes off easily enough". The heat was punctuated with terrific storms that would lash the trees and the fragile house. One morning early, as Maybeth still slept, an earthquake shook the house. Since Maybeth's bed was simply a small wooden framed cot, she presumed the wind was whistling around the corners and cracks in the house and shaking her bed. She was soon wakened more thoroughly by Agnes in her nightclothes who came running into her room, long hair streaming behind her, and asked if she had felt the earthquake. "Oh, is that what it was?" asked Maybeth sleepily and dropped back to sleep. God had given her a nature that did not fear, but had learned to trust. In a July 1937 letter to her father she wrote.

We have had more excitement this week, in the form of troubles in the house- scorpions! We have been having a southwest wind, and that always brings the scorpions out, they say. We have killed four in Agnes' room already! They are most of them quite small ones, and harmless, I guess – but we have had the fun of killing them! One night we found a big one right on the top of the wall, and we couldn't reach it without a ladder, so we called the two Chinese women in the house to come up and bring a ladder with them. They were all in their night attire and we were in ours – so we must have looked a lovely sight, all dancing around the room, in our pajamas and gowns, climbing ladders and waving the captured scorpion!

Daily work in the church helped the two young women improve their Chinese. Besides the demon possession problem, another roadblock to understanding was the extreme poverty and illiteracy of the people. As soon as one became a Christian, though, the new believer would save up enough pennies to buy a hymnbook. Hymnbooks were cheaper than Bibles and if one is illiterate it doesn't matter which book one has.

In the August 1937 issue of the Mission news magazine, *China's Millions*, Maybeth described the scene in their little church.

Our Sunday afternoon service is held in a very plain-looking place, with no stained-glass windows, carpets, or comfortable seats. We sit on hard benches with no backs to them – for two hours too! In the balcony I sit with the nearly eighty women, arriving early to get a good seat. Down below us there is just a sea of bobbing heads and a hum of voices broken now and then by a child's voice crying out.

There must be about four hundred in the building altogether – and we have to sit tightly. Most are poor country folk. Their clothing is often patched, and over their heads the women tie plain washcloths dyed black. Many of the women have walked in from their country homes on tiny little bound feet, though a few have been fortunate enough to ride - but such a rough springless ride on a wheelbarrow!

The service begins after we have been able to effect order out of chaos. Now everybody is finally seated, and the singing is about to start. When the number of the hymn is announced, the missionaries are showered with hymnbooks and asked to find the place. Most of these folk cannot read, but they insist upon having the book open at the right place!...The singing has plenty of volume but nothing of what we would call harmony or unity. But it is just thrilling to hear it, for it is a song of praise to the Lord, and He does not ask that our worship be tuneful or harmonious, but that it be in spirit and in truth – and many of these people do fulfill that condition. I wonder how the Lord feels as He sees these redeemed souls, snatched from heathen darkness and the clutch of Satan, now singing of Him and of the blood of Jesus Christ, which cleanses from all sin. My eyes fill with tears during that first hymn.

CHAPTER SIX

After her assignment to Lienshui, Maybeth wrote to a dear friend in Vancouver, Esther Bushy, who had been a great confidant to many of the young people preparing to go to China, telling her of her disappointment in being assigned to such an established church and not having the chance to be a true pioneer, but also of her confidence that the will of the Lord was "good, acceptable, and perfect." Hearing the same tone in a letter from Ken Gray, another new Canadian missionary, Esther Bushy suggested to Ken that he write Maybeth. Soon after she arrived in Lienshui, Maybeth received a note from Ken, one of the five men who had come out to China in 1936. It was just a short note, but a thoughtful one

His note said, "I heard through Esther Bushy that you were disappointed, and so I thought I'd write you a note. I've been designated to Chenghsien (Shengzhou), a city south of Shanghai along the coast, near Ningbo in a Bible teaching ministry and I've been really disappointed, but God has given me a verse, ' The will of the Lord is good, acceptable, and perfect.'" And he said, "I am so happy here. I'm working with a Welshman, Jack Sharman, and we're really having a great time working together."

Maybeth wrote back and said, "Of course, it's right. I'm very happy here. I just love the work in this station. I love my co-worker and I've really seen God work in a wonderful way that I'd never seen Him work before or since." She told him of the work of God's spirit in that city under the Chinese pastor, Mr. Chu. She described Mr. Chu, a short, slight man, gentle and godly, with a little wispy beard that hung down to his chest.

The Japanese War had escalated in the North and before the end of 1937 it spread to the east coast of China and almost to their doorstep, but Maybeth was very happy in Lienshui, learning the language and working with Agnes among the women in the city. She wrote to her father every week assuring him that, no matter what he heard or read in the newspapers, she was well and safe where she was.

Meanwhile she received another letter from Ken Gray telling of his work in Chenghsien. She found his letters very interesting and wrote back telling of the work she loved in Lienshui. This correspondence continued and over time the letters got longer and longer and sweeter and sweeter. Finally, after a year of correspondence, Maybeth received a letter from Ken in which he said, "I think we should combine our ministries."

Maybeth had no doubt about what he really meant because there was no way to combine a ministry of a woman and a man in China unless they were married! So, using her heart and her head, she jumped to the logical conclusion that this was a proposal. Ken always said that it was never meant that way, and Ken would tease Maybeth the rest of their lives about her railroading him into marriage.

Assuming he meant marriage, she wrote back and said, "I'm sorry, it's impossible; I can't cook." She had been brought up in boarding schools, mission schools, and mission stations and had very few child-hood opportunities to learn to keep a house or cook.

But he wrote back and said, "That's no problem; I can cook." And as it turned out, he was a very good cook. Ken was the youngest of a farm family of three boys in Alberta, Canada. He used to cook often on their farm; his mother was a semi-invalid and he had to cook many of the meals at the farm. When the family had threshing gangs and other large groups of people and had to cook pies and cakes and great quantities of food for the threshing gangs, Ken was the cook.

Before they could catch their breath, Ken and Maybeth were secretly engaged, telling no one else about it apart from their co-workers whom they swore to secrecy. They told God that they didn't want to rush into marriage unless He directly led it, and they also didn't want to announce their engagement without even enjoying one date together. Maybeth had seen so many apparent mistakes on the mission field, people who married in a hurry to avoid the loneliness, or people who married because they were afraid that, without a partner, life would be unbearable in

China. So there had been misfits, perhaps no more than there are in the homeland, but nevertheless difficult marriages did exist.

Maybeth and Ken prayed that if God wanted them together, He would bring them together from two provinces of China, but they would not give any inkling to the Mission authorities about their mutual interests. They trusted that if God did bring them together, their marriage would have His blessing.

Kenneth Thomas Gray did not have the long history of missionary work in his family, and his going to China as a missionary was not what many would have expected. Born the youngest son of three boys on a dairy farm outside of Calgary, Canada, Ken was raised in a home that honored the name of Christ. He attended church faithfully, but spent his youth in service to himself.

Ken wrote in the monthly magazine of the CIM soon after he had been accepted for missionary work in China,

As I look forward to a life of service for the Lord in China, my heart is greatly encouraged and strengthened as I consider His faithfulness in dealing with me. It is because of His great faithfulness that I am now on my way to China. God gave me Christian parents who have never ceased to pray for me. How I do praise Him for the restraining influence of their lives and prayers.

Living in the country, I escaped many of the snares which entrap young people today, and God in His faithfulness did not suffer me to go far into the pleasures of sin but, at the age of nineteen, arrested my wandering footsteps and started me in the path of obedience. I no doubt would have turned back if I had been left to myself, but the Lord shut out all possibility of retreat and left only the right way open.... The martyrdom of John and Betty Stam (CIM missionaries killed in the Boxer Rebellion in the early 1900's) and the sore need of young men for service in China were two outstanding factors which led me to apply to the China Inland Mission.

God knew my tendency to fear, so He has given me one of His sure words of promise upon which I rest with confidence: "Fear thou not; for I am with thee: be not dismayed; for I am thy God: I will strengthen

thee; yea, I will help thee; yea, I will uphold thee with the right hand of my righteousness." Isaiah 41:10.

As the years of their first term stretched on, both Ken and Maybeth would have many opportunities to prove God's faithfulness in their lives.

At the moment the chances of their even meeting for a day were slim. The country between them was embroiled in the war with the Japanese. Because of the war situation, the consulates and the Mission had told missionaries all over China that, because travel was so dangerous, nobody was to leave his or her assigned station. China and Japan were struggling for control of the Yangtze River, and few missionaries could travel without using the rivers.

So Maybeth and Ken concluded that what they most wanted might have to wait until such time as God wanted them to be married. He would have to bring Ken up from the South and Maybeth down from the North to a mutual meeting place, so that they'd have at least one date before they got married. They left it in God's hands and continued to correspond.

CHAPTER SEVEN

Meanwhile as the summer of 1937 wore on, the war began to heat up. The armies of Japan and China were engaged in northeastern China, where much territory was under Japanese control. The Japanese had also seized a large area along the coast and around Shanghai where the CIM mission headquarters was. Chang Kai-Shek and his Nationalist government attacked the Japanese garrison in Shanghai in August of 1937 in what became one of the bloodiest battles of the war. It was a battle of human resource against the technical resources of the Japanese. Chinese casualties amounted to hundreds of thousands of soldiers as the Japanese marshaled their air force and navy against the Chinese army. Since at this time there were no Allied powers aligned with China, missionaries were nominally safe as neutral parties. Those who were in the Japanese occupied sections of Shanghai, however, and the provinces in the North were still vulnerable to the same plight of many Chinese civilians whose homes were bombed and families killed by the invading Japanese. Many supposedly neutral missionary families suffered imprisonment and harm from the occupying Japanese army.

A call to prayer went out from the pages of the *China's Millions*, the CIM monthly newsletter: *"Already the casualties on both sides have been huge, consisting not only of soldiers but also of innocent non-combatants who have been the victims of bombing and shelling operations carried out on a sweeping scale by the invaders. There has also been wanton destruction of property, aggregating in Shanghai alone hundreds of millions of dollars in value. The fighting grows fiercer each succeeding day, and no one can predict what the end will be."*

While the leaders of the CIM asked missionaries to stay in the cities where they were working, Japanese troops were plying the Yangtze

River pushing toward Nanking, the Nationalist Chinese capitol at the time. Maybeth and Agnes continued on with their work, occasionally hearing bombing at nearby cities. They received the Shanghai paper, but often several days late, and so they believed that most of the fighting was in the North. It was a surprise, therefore, one night when news came to them that they must not light their lamps that night. Expecting bombing and strafing from planes, they went to bed with some concern, but still convinced that they were in the hollow of God's hand and that He would bring nothing their way that was not for His glory. Nothing happened that night. The following few days more news came, some of it rumor and some of it the truth.

Lienshui city officials believed that their city was in a rather important position for the Japanese on their way to Nanking. The canal, dug in the recent past, made a clear passage from Tsiang-Kiang-pu (Huaiyin) to Lienshui, right past the city walls, and on to the ocean and was deep enough for warships to negotiate. News reached Maybeth and Agnes that some Japanese warships were at the mouth of the canal planning to come up to TKP, (Maybeth's abbreviation for Tsiang-Kiang-pu), Lienshui's nearest city to the south. TKP was directly connected to Nanking both by canal and by a road that had just been completed. Apparently the Chinese, realizing the danger, had stationed 18 fighter planes in TKP to guard the mouth of the canal. Daily Maybeth and Agnes could watch the Chinese planes making surveillance runs along the route of the canal and right past the city walls.

The two young women could not help being affected by the atmosphere in the city. Rumors of war were rampant, though, and at every rumor of approaching Japanese bombers, many Chinese would panic and make wild plans of fleeing the city and running off to the country, where it was presumed it would be safer. Although Maybeth and Agnes tried to stay calm, their fears were rising. By December 1937 the Japanese had conquered the Yangtze River valley to Nanking where they unleashed their frustration against stubborn Chinese resistance by killing and raping in a scene unimaginable in modern history. The story of the Nanking massacre reached Maybeth and Agnes and they learned of the horrific events that had taken place in that city when the Japanese reached it. Mercifully they did not know the details of the looting, raping, torturing and murdering that had taken place.

The reputation of foreigners was, according to most Chinese that they would fly at the first sign of trouble. Such an opinion was borne out one day when some of the residents of the town questioned the Nationalist Chinese soldiers, who manned the gate of the city, if the Japanese were on the way. The soldiers commented, "You don't need to get excited over this affair as yet. Why, the foreigners are still in the city, and you can be sure that if it was really serious, they would have left the city long ago." Maybeth and Agnes determined then that they would stay as long as they possibly could, hoping that meant through the whole war. It was not to be.

A system of warning was set up in the city consisting of a large bell at the gate of the city which would be rung twice if Japanese planes were approaching and then beat continuously if it was necessary to leave the houses and run into the country. The bell was near the mission compound and since their house was larger than most in the city, they paid close attention, knowing that their house would make an obvious target.

Maybeth wrote to her father of the political situation and apparent impending war.

China definitely seems to be preparing for a real war, and if so, I don't see how we will be able to stay here in the interior. I understand that China has borrowed a lot from America, both money and planes, and now America is sending out 200 aeroplane pilots and mechanics! I think that China should do something to Japan soon – instead of just sitting and letting her take all her country away from her without saying a thing.... I understand the Reds up North are laying down their arms of rebellion and they are joining up with the government army like they ought to.

She expressed wishes that many already felt. Mao Tse-Tung had indeed joined forces with Chiang Kai-Shek, but Chiang, short handed and lacking support, was playing a waiting game, it seemed. He was waiting for foreign governments to join him in the fight with the Japanese and until then was only engaging the Japanese when there was no other option.

One morning as Agnes and Maybeth were preparing the house for guests for the week, a young woman who lived across the street from them came to visit. She had been Agnes's teacher when she had first arrived in Lienshui, a lovely, educated, modern young lady from a wealthy family. Maybeth thought how lovely she looked, as she stood in the doorway in a long flowered, voile gown with very short sleeves and a high stiff collar. She wanted to know when they were planning to evacuate and urged them to be ready to leave at a moment's notice. Her family had a radio and she told them of the bombing of Shanghai and the burning of large parts of the city. Her family was planning to leave the city to go to their country home where most believed it would be safer.

Maybeth's letter to her father in August of 1937, told of the uncertainty of the world around her, but she added,

We're not worried about things at all, but just wondering how it is all going to develop. It is hard to settle down to read and study though, when folks will keep coming in with fresh reports and rumours about the affairs of the war and how things are going here in China. Agnes and I will study for a while, and then she will come into my room and talk for a while, and then we'll study again for a bit more, and then more discussion as to what we'd take with us, if we did have to go, and what we would do with the things that we'd leave behind. It really is hard to know what would be the most necessary things to take.

Near the end of August, Maybeth and Agnes received an express letter from the consul in Shanghai informing them that they should be ready to leave at a moment's notice. The war situation was getting more and more unstable. Maybeth and Agnes packed up their belongings, but stayed to work as long as possible.

Finally at the beginning of September 1937, the CIM office told Maybeth and Agnes to move down to the station directly south of them, TKP, soon to be renamed Huaiyin, where a missionary family lived and worked. Two single ladies in such a dangerous place was simply asking for trouble, the Mission leaders believed, and they would be safer in the home of Mr. and Mrs. Carlburg in TKP. Believing that the war situation was only temporary, Maybeth and Agnes cycled down to TKP, about 20 miles south. There they stayed with Ernest and Geneva Carlburg, an American couple and their three little boys.

PART TWO – WAR AND RUMOR OF WAR

"Fear not I am with thee; O be not afraid.
For I am Thy God and will still give thee aid
I'll strengthen thee, help thee, and cause thee to stand
Upheld by My righteous, omnipotent hand."

CHAPTER EIGHT

Mail was erratic and sometimes a month or two would go by before Maybeth heard from her parents. Charles, her father, was very particular about writing to her frequently, but the letters would get held up somewhere in China and then would come through six or seven at a time. Sometimes, the isolation was hard. Sometimes when the mail arrived and there was still no letter from her father, her heart sank and she felt very alone. Messages from the consul and from the Mission headquarters would cross or arrive in the wrong order, one message saying to evacuate and the next saying to stay where they were.

They did hear of the terrible bombings of Shanghai by both the Japanese and the Chinese planes. As the Chinese pulled out of Shanghai that August, they set fire to almost half of the city, a conflagration considered by some historians to be one of the most massive in history. Through it all, however, the CIM headquarters was not harmed, although at one time a bomb fell on it, lodged between two close walls and failed to detonate. God's protective hand seemed to be guarding the CIM family.

Evacuation really was not possible since the Chinese had mined the rivers and canals to prevent Japanese gun ships from using them. That meant that there was no commercial travel on the rivers or canals and the price of a rickshaw was outrageous. With the added demand, rickshaw drivers were becoming the new wealthy.

Because of the upheaval, Maybeth and Agnes rode their bicycles many times that fall the 20 miles between TKP and Lienshui, always believing that the instability would dissipate and they would be able to return to Lienshui for good. No sooner would they make the ride back to Lienshui, but there would be a message from the Mission asking them to return to TKP. Sometimes it looked as though they could evacuate to Shanghai, but then a new Japanese offensive would keep them where they were. When they made the bicycle trip to Lienshui, Japanese bombers often flew over the road, strafing as they went and there was no place to hide except in the ditches alongside the road. Maybeth and Agnes dropped their bicycles and dived into the ditches and fields alongside the road until the planes were past. Once, Maybeth wrote to her father,

Just after we got out of the city of TKP, - planes came and circled over the city. The people on the road made us get off our cycles and hide with them among the sunflowers. We did and it was quite fun. Once I fell ankle deep into a lovely mud-puddle!

Maybeth and a friend cover the miles between mission stations on the only available transportation: bicycles.

Life in TKP soon began to develop a pattern. Each morning, Japanese bombers would fly over the city and drop many bombs. When the temple bells would start ringing as warning that bombers were approaching, Maybeth and Agnes and the Carlburg family would all file down to the basement, sometimes holding their breakfast toast in hand, and wait until the bombing was over.

Maybeth was so impressed by the calm manner in which Mrs. Carlburg dealt with her little boys, never showing fear or in any way causing them to panic. The little boys would exclaim every time they heard a plane fly low over the house. Sometimes it was fairly near and they could hear the bombs dropping, and then they would say in a fascinated voice, "There goes one, Mommy" and "There goes another one!" Their parents were careful to never let them be fearful of the bombing, only interested. Then when the planes had passed over and the all-clear signal would sound everyone would go back upstairs and carry on with the regular routine of the day. Mr. Carlburg and the two young women would go out into the city to see if they could help the injured or homeless. This pattern was repeated each day. Sometimes the bombs were close, but never did they cause any harm to the house.

One night they were invited to the other side of the city to the home of Nelson Bell and his wife, missionaries with the Southern Presbyterian church. Dr. Bell had a daughter, Ruth, who would later become the wife of noted evangelist Billy Graham. They lived in a better part of the city in a beautiful compound which was entirely American. They had a lovely big stone house with a swimming pool. As Maybeth and Agnes stepped in the door, it was like stepping into a piece of America, planted in the middle of China.

Dr. Bell had a large hospital nearby and he was very much loved and almost worshipped in that area. A very godly man, he carried on evangelistic work along with his medical work. Maybeth and Agnes were invited for American Thanksgiving in November. It was a wonderful treat to step into their beautiful American home and enjoy a big turkey dinner. Dr. Bell, with his surgeon's skill carved the turkey and Mrs. Bell was a gracious host.

The Bells had many starts and stops before they were able to safely leave TKP. Dr. Bell received telegrams from the American ambassador in Shanghai at the rate of about two or three a day with the latest evacuation reports. The British missionaries found an occasion to joke about it with him, because each of the telegrams seemed to contradict the previous one just received. When the consul ordered them to evacuate, Dr. Bell wrote a telegram back asking that he not evacuate until it was absolutely necessary. He was given dates when he could meet an American destroyer at the port of Haichow about 84 miles north, and he chose the last date. In the meantime, however, the Japanese moved gunboats, and even an aircraft carrier, into Haichow harbor blocking entrance to American ships.

Maybeth wrote to her father,

Every day this past week, these missionaries have had different plans for their leaving – always according to the news that they received by telegram from their consulate. One day they were leaving the following day, only to be told when that day arrived that the Japanese had blocked that route. So they thought of another route for the next day, and the next day that route was blocked too. After he had left his home, planning to take the boat part of the way and then take the train, he [Dr. Bell] received a telegram at his house telling him that he could meet the destroyer at Haichow now. Of course there was no way he could get to Haichow immediately. It is at least a day and a half trip.

Meanwhile, many of the CIM missionaries stayed in TKP and wondered what the future held as they saw their fellow missionaries leaving for safer places. Geneva Carlburg considered taking the children and leaving also, but decided to wait for further developments. Maybeth and Agnes, meanwhile, were making plans to return to Lienshui. They had received word that a great friend and fine preacher, Mr. Orr, was willing to come to Lienshui for an autumn conference for the church there. Maybeth wrote excitedly to her father about this possibility.

We'll be so glad if he does come up, for he is certainly a blessing in Lienshui when he comes up there. It will be so good to get back 'home' in Lienshui again. We have certainly missed the folks since we left there, and we do long to be back among them again. We'd like to stay right on with them, even if there is trouble, for after all, we didn't come out to China because we thought that it was the safest place in the world!

Maybeth and Agnes rode their bicycles back to Lienshui and prepared for the coming autumn conference in the church there. They immediately noticed differences in the city. The city government had built a high watchtower from which a watchman could telephone other cities as part of the air raid warning system across the country.

They had also dug holes in the bank on each side of the canal and told the townspeople that in the event of a serious bombing, they were to crawl into these holes in the bank. The holes were quite small and Maybeth imagined what might be lurking in the back of them. When it rained one day, she imagined crawling into one of those holes filled with muddy water and refuse. She and Agnes decided they'd take their chances in the open country around the city.

Travel was dangerous, though, because the preoccupation of the government with the war with Japan allowed bandits to roam the country with little interference. The women heard of several country homes that had been robbed.

The Chinese doctor who lived across the street from Maybeth and Agnes invited the women to come across and listen to the evening news from London on his radio. They thought that was a great idea, but it seemed that every time the hour approached, the air raid alarm would ring and they would have to stay in their houses and put their lights out. News, therefore, was scarce.

In October 1937, amid trips back and forth from Lienshui to TKP, Agnes and Maybeth hosted the autumn conference with the much-loved guest speaker, Mr. Orr. There were eight baptisms in the Lienshui church and a great time of rejoicing.

Some of the Lienshui women, however, tearfully told Maybeth that the Chinese Army had demanded a son from each family in the city and had taken them away for training. The old Chinese pastor informed Maybeth and Agnes that there were more and more Chinese soldiers in the town and that the Chinese commander had his eye on their house for accommodations for the soldiers.

51

Maybeth and Agnes had been trying to prevent their occupation of the house by frequently visiting Lienshui, but it was obvious that they could not continue to do that with winter coming on. It seemed apparent that they were going to have to stay in TKP for the foreseeable future, so, reluctantly, they moved everything of value to TKP and the home of the Carlburgs. By Maybeth's 24th birthday at the end of October, the two women had been sent down to TKP for good, they believed. They still held out hope that the war situation would pass them by and they would be able to return, but such plans for the near future looked bleak.

CHAPTER NINE

Later that fall, confirming their belief, the British government sent the Carlburgs and Maybeth and Agnes a telegram and informed them that there was too much bombing going on in the city (and there was a good deal) and it was too dangerous, so they were to go to Shanghai. The plan was that they were to make their way down the small river tributary nearby until it met the Yangtze River. The Yangtze had been taken over by the Japanese, but the British consul said that he would arrange for a small British gunboat to meet them at the junction of the tributary and the Yangtze and take them down to Shanghai.

It was exciting; it was especially exciting for Maybeth because she reckoned she'd be that much nearer Ken. She would be coming from the north coastal area to the more central coastal area of China. So the Carlburgs and Agnes and Maybeth made plans to leave. The warnings of the British consul were confirmed by the leaders of the CIM who thought it best that with three small children and two unmarried ladies, it would be safer to move all of them to Shanghai.

Mr. Carlburg hired a tiny little boat and they put their meager baggage in it. The boat was just big enough for five Carlburgs, Agnes and Maybeth and a couple boatmen to lie down flat at night. Because there was so much danger of the boys falling overboard, the Carlburgs tied a rope around each boy and tied the rope to the mast in the middle. Then, if they slipped over the side or fell over reaching into the water, they could be hauled back into the boat.

The little river was packed with activity: thousands of houseboats and cargo boats sailed back and forth continually. Many Chinese lived on houseboats without any home on land. As the first night approached, all eight passengers lay down side by side in the bottom of the boat and tried to get some sleep as one of the boatmen steered the boat down the river. There was only just enough room and no thrashing around or even rolling over was possible.

Several days later they arrived at the point where the tributary met the Yangtze River. On that day, Geneva Carlburg had been doing a huge washing and instead of putting a sail up in the boat, she used the mast to hang diapers. So the little boat boasted a long string of diapers starting at the front and going right up to the top of the mast and then back down to the back of the boat. Diapers were flapping everywhere as they reached the junction of the Yangtze, and, sure enough, a British gun boat was waiting for them and a British consul came on board their boat, dodging wet diapers as he came, to talk to them in the bottom of the boat.

He graciously arranged for them to come on board the gunboat. It really wasn't a big ship with no accommodations for them to sleep. They planned to live on the boat during the day and then go ashore at night, stay at a British hotel, and be protected by the troops that were on the ship. The weeklong trip proved exciting; as they went down the river they would see Japanese ships often, but since they were flying a British flag, they were left alone. Britain was not yet in the war; it was a Japanese/Chinese war at that point and Britain was a third party and neutral, simply protecting her own citizens. British boats had been fired upon, however, and so tension was high when Japanese boats, manned by soldiers, came near.

The little party finally reached Shanghai to be met by the rest of the CIM folks. The Mission compound was fairly crowded because refugees had come from other areas. Shanghai itself was a teeming, overcrowded refugee city.

Maybeth was given lovely living quarters while in Shanghai. Her friends among the secretaries for the Mission directors were people who knew her father well, and so they asked if, instead of crowding her into the Mission home where hundreds of other missionaries were packed, they could share a spare room in their apartment complex with Maybeth. She felt spoiled, but she loved the accommodations. She had a nice little room there all to herself instead of having to share with others in the Mission house. The secretaries were all good to her, mostly because they remembered her as a child. Maybeth's father had been secretary-treasurer of the CIM in Shanghai. She enjoyed their company and the seclusion of their apartment complex.

Because of her secret engagement, Maybeth's situation was a bit unusual anyway. Although she could have used the time in Shanghai to work on her language study, she knew that if she married Ken, she would be moved to another Mission station and would have to learn a different dialect. A distance of seventy or eighty miles in China could mean a different dialect completely, barely understandable by those outside the region. Maybeth, of course, didn't tell anyone of her hopes, but her language study was a bit half-hearted and she was glad to volunteer to work among the refugees on the University of Shanghai campus.

Shanghai University had been closed to all classes and the university campus had been turned into an enormous refugee camp. Japanese forces had taken all the country around Shanghai and so the people who were afraid of the soldiers had swarmed into the city believing there would be more protection there. The upper class part of the city, where the university was located, did indeed provide some protection since it included the International Concession which was off limits to the Japanese army. Thousands of refugees had flocked to this large group of brick buildings and filled the buildings to an unhealthy degree. Because there was such need of help and because there were many missionaries who had also fled to Shanghai, many volunteered to help in this temporary refugee camp. Different mission societies and denominations were represented and they all worked together to serve the helpless and hopeless.

When Maybeth arrived at the university campus to volunteer at the refugee camp, the organizers were skeptical of what a young woman with few language skills would be able to do, but finally they found a job they thought she could handle if she was still willing.

"We hope you won't mind taking this job. We can't even get a Chinese to take it."

"What is it?" she asked.

"Delouse these garments," they said pointing to a pile of vermin-infested garments. Because of the heat, the lice were multiplying quickly.

A large delousing machine existed on the premises, but it didn't work properly. Sometimes the steam did nothing more than just stun the lice. Maybeth's job was to go over all the garments and pick off all the lice, the live and the dead, and drop them into a pail of insecticide. Shortly thereafter, the delousing machine completely broke down, so two or three of the missionaries worked on the refugees' clothing by hand. It was an unpleasant job, but Maybeth held to the theory that if one takes a job that is really bad, that no one else wants to do, then after that nothing seems to be a bad job. She quickly decided that, since no one had given her a choice, it was a good idea to start at the bottom.

Another girl, Minnie Klep, and Maybeth worked together for a while. Minnie was a little older than Maybeth and they were able to find fun working together. They worked about three days a week, and when Maybeth got back to her room at the end of one of those days, she'd fill the bathtub to the brim with water and soak herself in it hoping to drown any errant lice that had jumped over to her.

Meanwhile Maybeth continued corresponding with Ken. He knew that she was in Shanghai now, but still he felt strongly that he should not ask to come up to Shanghai. He was only a day's journey southwest by boat from Shanghai, but Ken was never one to ask for privileges, and he and Maybeth planned to trust God. Ken had testified that God had shown His faithfulness to him in bringing him to salvation and in sending him to China. He had said in his initial testimonial in the *China's Millions*, when he was sent to China, "I look forward to new experiences with my Lord in China. I rejoice in the fact that He will not suffer His faithfulness to fail; His covenant He will not break; nor will He alter the thing that is gone out of His lips." They had prayed that God would bring them together and they didn't want to manipulate the circumstances in any way. So they decided to continue corresponding and trust in their God's faithfulness.

They did not have long to wait. One day, only a month or so later, at the daily early morning prayer meeting in the CIM home, a prayer request was made for a young new worker who hadn't been well of late, Ken Gray. The doctor down in his mission station had recommended that he come up to Shanghai for some more treatment and a checkup. He was to arrive in the next couple of days by boat. Maybeth's heart began to pound with excitement. The rest of the prayer requests for the day were quickly forgotten as she thought of seeing Ken at last. The illness didn't sound serious enough to cause her alarm. Not only had the Lord gloriously answered her prayer in bringing them together, but she was also going to have that long-awaited date in the next few days.

Maybeth still did not tell anyone her secret, but she did manage to find out which boat he was arriving on and met him at the pier. She was the only person meeting the boat and her feelings were conflicted and confused. Here was a man whom she had never dated, to whom she was practically engaged, and there he was, standing on the deck, waving.

Maybeth had had a horrible suspicion while she was writing to him that she was taller than Ken and she foolishly thought she would be very embarrassed to have a husband who was shorter than she was. Whatever the case, little could be done now and there he was smiling broadly as the ship pulled into the harbor. Maybeth, a bit hesitantly, went over to the end of the gangplank and met him as he came down.

Ken practically ran down the gangplank and immediately threw his arms around her and enveloped her in a big hug. They hugged and kissed, somewhat more discreetly, on the street car on the way back to the Mission home and by the time they arrived, they had decided that this streetcar ride was enough of a date and they could announce their engagement. Maybeth was still not sure if she was taller than he was, but somehow it didn't matter now. As it later became apparent, they were almost exactly the same height.

Ken went into the hospital in Shanghai with a minor kidney infection that was very easily diagnosed and cured. In two or three days he was well again, and he and Maybeth were able to spend a few days together there in Shanghai. Maybeth thought it was very exciting; everybody seemed surprised. The exception was Esther Bushy who had suggested that they write and had an inkling of what was going on.

Maybeth had known about Ken before leaving for the mission field. She had been living in the Mission home in Philadelphia when Ken had come through that home as a candidate in the fall of 1936. She had already been accepted to go to China from Vancouver that fall, but was visiting her parents while the men were attending candidate school. Ken came to candidate school from Western Canada, from Prairie Bible Institute, a school Maybeth had also attended. She had seen him when she was in her last year of Bible School. He was a freshman and Maybeth was a senior. At Prairie Bible Institute the women didn't talk with the men, nor did they attempt to make any dates since it was not their purpose for attending the school. Students were there to study the Bible and no distractions were encouraged. Ken, at the time, thought Maybeth was a very stuck-up English girl who wouldn't talk to anybody.

Maybeth, in her later years would explain,

Actually "stuck-up" is often the tag people put on others who are excessively shy and I was rather a shy person, nor was I out to particularly win any men. Ken and another fellow used to play piano duets. They would put two pianos back to back and play wonderfully. I thought Ken was a cocky sort of guy; he obviously loved playing the piano, loved accompanying hymns at the church. So my whole view of him was of a very talented, cocky sort of a kid. When he came down to Philadelphia as a candidate, he was somewhat interested in another girl who was a candidate with the Mission also.

While they were going to candidate classes, Maybeth helped around the home. The Mission employed two black women to help in the home at that time, Mabel and Virginia. Mabel was a large smiling woman who did most of the cooking. She was consistently good-natured and everyone was fond of her. Virginia cleaned house and helped with setting the table and serving meals. Virginia, for some unknown reason, had a notion that Ken and Maybeth were the ones that should be together. Everyone who ate meals in the house had his own napkin ring, and when Virginia put the napkins around the table, she would always put Maybeth's beside Ken's. Maybeth used to get a little provoked at her; she thought she had the nerve to always try to shove them together. "Ken had said that he was interested in another girl, so why would he be interested in her?" she thought. And because he had another interest, Maybeth wasn't even looking at him. So soon after Virginia had set the table, Maybeth would slip down into the dining room and move the napkins so that she was no longer next to Ken. But Virginia caught on and she would come in just before the last bell for dinner rang and switch them back again. For weeks Virginia and Maybeth had a running battle about the napkin rings. Maybeth remembered that Virginia used to get so excited when she had the last shot and Maybeth would be beside Ken. Apparently Virginia saw something that escaped both Ken and Maybeth.

Ken Gray thought of himself as a simple Western boy without sophistication and feared that he would not be enough of a man of God for someone with Maybeth's credentials. After all, her grandfather was one of the first missionaries to come to China with Hudson Taylor, the founder of the China Inland Mission, and her father and mother were active members of the CIM, hosting the home in Philadelphia. All the old-timers in the Mission knew her and remembered her from childhood. It was a little intimidating. He wrote to his great friend, Lem Fowler, in Calgary, Alberta about his concerns.

I am at last in Shanghai with a few days behind and a few more ahead of me to enjoy the presence of one who means a whole lot to me these days. She is a grand girl, and the best of it is, that the more I get to know of Maybeth, the better she is, and the more I have to thank the Lord for His leading. Do pray, Lem, that I may be what she desires in her man. I do feel that I am so far behind her in so many things, yet it is only as the grace of God works in my life that I can be anything.... However, I know you will be with me in prayer that I may appropriate the grace of God to such an extent that Maybeth will never regret the step she has taken. After all it [agreeing to marry me] is no light matter... and I know she has not done it lightly, but I do desire that she may be more and more satisfied with ...me.

Maybeth's engagement meant that she had to begin to learn the Ningbo dialect so that she could be understood in the area where Ken was working. Ken, meanwhile, had returned to his Mission station, Chenghsien (Shengzhou) to continue the work with his friend, Jack Sharman. Maybeth's language study was to be taken in the Ningbo area and she was sent to work on a Mission station with Miss Dorothy Beugler, who Maybeth thought was "just a peach." She was a lovely, single lady missionary who kept up with the times by reading the newspaper in Chinese everyday. Generally, missionary ladies in China never learned to read the newspaper, but Miss Beugler was not to be bound by tradition. Maybeth had a delightful six months with her and came to admire her understanding of the Chinese people and her love for them.

CHAPTER TEN

Ken had been told by the Mission that after they were married they would be working in Fenghua, a mission station over the mountains and east of Chenghsien, the city where he had been working with Jack Sharman. Ken asked if he could go to the new mission station early and settle in there so that when he got married he would be used to the work there. The Mission agreed and Ken went to Fenghua, taking with him a young Chinese couple. The man was a local farmer boy, non-Christian, but a very fine young man, Boh Jing, and his new wife, Jing Shang. Boh Jing said he wanted to learn how to be a foreign cook, and Ken, sensitive to Maybeth's fear of the responsibility of cooking, thought that he would train Boh Jing to cook the kind of food he liked, do a little canning and preserving, and when Maybeth arrived, she would have someone who already knew how to cook.

As Ken and the young Chinese couple worked together in Fenghua in those first few weeks and months, preparing the house for Maybeth's arrival, Ken talked with them about their spiritual need, and they became very earnest Christians and soon intensely loyal to Ken. A little struggling church existed in the city, and Ken worked in it, but in the evenings, he trained Boh Jing to cook. Boh Jing was an apt pupil and soon he could make such delicacies as cheese soufflé, upside down cakes, roasts and side dishes to go with a great variety of food. Almost all missionaries in that day hired local people to work for them. The pay was not a great drain on the Mission finances, and it allowed missionaries more time for teaching and preaching. An added benefit to the local community was the opportunity for local residents to make more money than they could otherwise. The arrangement worked well and many Chinese came to know and love the God of their employers, as they worked alongside them and observed their lives.

Ken wrote to Maybeth explaining that when she arrived as the lady of the house, she would not be expected to cook. She would simply announce the day's menu to Boh Jing and he would make it. Ken would tell her what he could make and Maybeth could never let on that she didn't know how to cook. Meanwhile, Ken thought, she could concentrate on language study and working in the church. Maybeth, already apprehensive about the idea of running a household, thought that sounded like a great plan.

They had planned to be married in February and, as the time got nearer, they went to Shanghai to live for several weeks before the wedding, a stipulation of British law. Their planned wedding date was February 7. In 1939 in Shanghai, a couple could be legally married in the British cathedral, by the Anglican minister. Or they could get married at the British Consulate without much ceremony by what Maybeth viewed as the "old, stuffy" British Consul. Being married in the cathedral, which was a gorgeous Gothic building with stained glass windows, implied that the wedding couple and guests would have expensive wedding clothes and a whole retinue of attendants, something Maybeth and Ken couldn't afford or want. They wanted a simple wedding.

Money was scarce anyway, so they decided they wouldn't plan on a wedding at the cathedral. Ken had already been struggling with the idea of getting Maybeth an engagement ring. He didn't have enough money to buy her one, and Maybeth kept on insisting that she didn't need one. As she saw it, they were engaged and that was all that mattered. No engagement ring would prove anything they didn't already know, she said. But Ken felt very bad and wanted to give her a diamond.

One day he received a letter from his Canadian friend, Lem, with a gift of $20. When the money was exchanged for Chinese money, it made about $70. Seventy Chinese dollars was just the amount Ken needed for a simple diamond engagement ring. Not only had his friend Lem been praying for him, he had seen a need and had helped his old buddy out! Ken was thrilled. He went out and bought a very simple diamond engagement ring and surprised Maybeth with it.

Maybeth's sister, Kathy, gave Maybeth her wedding dress. Kathy was Maybeth's only sibling and they were very close. Kathy had returned to China also as a missionary and had recently gone back to the United States for her first furlough after serving a term in China. While she was in Philadelphia, where Maybeth's parents worked for the CIM at the time, she had married a British missionary, Leslie Lyall there. So Kathy sent the beautiful gown her father had bought for her. It fit perfectly and Maybeth borrowed someone else's veil and another friend's shoes. Ken bought himself a new suit and they did look handsome. Ken for years referred to that suit as his wedding suit, since it was the only good suit he had. That suit had to last for many years of desperate times after the wedding.

Gifts from home and nearby started to arrive as the news of their upcoming wedding spread. Those who couldn't send gifts sent them money, and Ken and Maybeth enjoyed the luxury of shopping in some of the fancy stores in Shanghai. As with all brides and grooms, they were excited about setting up their new home and through the generosity of friends were able to buy many things that appealed to them. One particular delight to Maybeth was the set of English dishes they bought, mostly blue, with a pattern that covered the plates. Maybeth, a child raised in boarding schools and Mission homes, had never had possessions that mattered to her and she felt so thrilled and privileged as she and Ken planned their first home.

The Mission owned a small house in Fenghua, so tiny it was called the "Mission matchbox." Maybeth and Ken were thrilled with the simplicity of the house, because they wanted to have a home where the Chinese could see everything, where nothing was hidden from them, and where they could feel comfortable. Many of the houses the CIM had acquired over the years were great huge old European styled houses which immediately intimidated the poverty-stricken Chinese.

Ken, much earlier, had sent a letter to Maybeth's father asking for her hand in marriage. It was not easy for him to ask this request of such an esteemed pioneer missionary. He anxiously awaited the reply and felt considerable relief when the telegram finally came through with Charles

Judd's approval. Maybeth's father also offered to send out wedding announcements; not a real invitation since it was impractical for most of their friends to be present at the wedding. On that announcement the wedding date was set for February 7. By February 3, however, Ken and Maybeth, anxious to be married and having fulfilled the government required time spent in Shanghai before the wedding, pushed the wedding forward four days. All those who could be in Shanghai were already there and there seemed no reason to delay.

The final plan was to get married at the British consulate in the morning and then have what they considered their REAL Christian wedding in the afternoon at the Mission home. For this second wedding they would dress in their wedding finery, and Mr. Warren, one of the beloved Mission directors, would marry them. Their reception would be right there in the same home and then they would go away on their honeymoon. Maybeth's mother and father had arranged with the supervisors of the home in Shanghai to provide anything they thought was appropriate for a wedding reception as their absentee gift for the young couple.

Obviously neither Maybeth's nor Ken's parents could be there, but Dr. and Mrs. Fred Judd, Maybeth's uncle and aunt, were in Shanghai and Dr. Judd gave her away. They had no bridesmaid, but opted instead for a little flower girl who was a distant relative of Maybeth's. Her name was Elizabeth Hoyt, about six years old. Maybeth had a tailor make her a little pink dress and she wore a wreath of flowers in her hair. She was very excited about being part of the wedding party. During the later upheaval that took China by storm, Elizabeth Hoyt was interned in a Japanese prison camp in Weihsien in Northern China for almost three years.

Early on the wedding day, Mrs. Judd, Maybeth's aunt, insisted that Maybeth have breakfast in bed and carried it up on a tray to her bedroom. Maybeth later described her as a "sweet old-fashioned lady." Then Dr. and Mrs. Judd and Ken and Maybeth drove over to the British Consulate to have the civil wedding ceremony. There was no dressing up for this wedding; they went over in ordinary clothes. The British Consul was, according to Maybeth, "a funny old fuddy-duddy; he mumbled and spluttered and it was hard to understand what he was saying." He announced that he was going to read a script and when he came to certain words he pointed out beforehand, Maybeth and Ken were to say, "I do." He mumbled on and spluttered over this script and afterwards Maybeth wondered if he really said anything, but he finally announced that they were married. It was the most dry and stuffy ceremony imaginable, but it was their legal marriage. The young people didn't even think of it as anything of importance though, certainly not a proper wedding; they knew that they were going to say their vows that afternoon.

Wedding photo taken outside the CIM Mission Home in Shanghai, Feb. 3, 1939. Left to right: Dr. Fred Judd, Ken Gray, Maybeth Gray, Dr. Warren, Edith Judd. Front: Elizabeth Hoyte

The real wedding was certainly simple. Maybeth in her borrowed finery and carrying a beautiful bouquet of lilies came down the long staircase on the arm of her uncle Fred. The excited little flower girl followed Maybeth down the staircase and at one moment Maybeth heard a tear as Elizabeth stepped on her floor length veil. No one noticed anything though, and after the wedding Maybeth couldn't even find anything amiss. She descended the stairs to the tune of a hymn and the couple recessed also to the tune of another hymn. They wanted things simple and personal. It wasn't the usual wedding music at all. People seemed quite pleased that they had done something different. They had consulted with Dr. Warren earlier about what they had planned: no wed-ding march or usual arrangements.

"Will people be shocked by it?" they asked.

"It'll do them good to be shocked." replied Dr. Warren, a kindly gentleman with a long bushy white beard, masses of white hair and very pink cheeks. He married them with due solemnity and all the gathered missionaries and their families enjoyed the reception afterwards in the dining room.

Maybeth wasn't interested in throwing her bouquet. It was so lovely with the lilies and little white flowers mixed in with the trailing fern. Instead, during the reception she slipped up to the top floor of the Mission home and gave her it away to one of the patients in the hospital there. Mrs. Knight had been the principal of the school when Maybeth had been at Chefoo and was dying of cancer. All the girls had loved her; she was a wonderful friend. She was so delighted when Maybeth burst into her room in all her wedding regalia and gave her the bouquet. The nurses put it over the mirror there in her hospital room where it trailed beautifully and she could see it from her bed.

The honeymoon location was a secret, though everyone knew it wouldn't be very far away. Ken had decided to use a hotel for four or five days in a part of Shanghai that had been taken over by the Japanese. The Mission home and all the places they had been up to that time in Shanghai were in the British Concession, an area that was like a little island of England and had not been taken by the Japanese. The only way to the honeymoon hotel was to cross a river, crowded with little Chinese boats, out of the British Concession and into the Japanese held section. It was a large modern hotel, but seldom used by Europeans for fear of trouble with the Japanese. Ken had made inquiries and was able to have their safety assured and a very cheap rate as well.

The only snag in Maybeth's mind was that when they got to the edge of the bridge across the river, they were required to bow to the Japanese guards. Maybeth stubbornly refused to bow, but Ken, always the pragmatist, did. In their passage back and forth on the bridge, he would do the bowing and Maybeth would follow in behind him. At the hotel a servant showed them to a lovely room and as the sun set they stood in the room at the window looking out over Shanghai and thinking how wonderful it was to be married. They were delighted that the wedding had gone off so well, that God had brought them together, and that they had one another.

The honeymoon was a time for them to enjoy time together, something they had experienced very little so far, and they went out now and again to explore in that part of Shanghai. The Mission home had been in that area when Maybeth was a child growing up there, and so she took Ken down the familiar streets and showed him all her favorite haunts in that part of Shanghai, which was now practically all Japanese territory. The Japanese always treated them very well as they were third party nationals.

Oddly enough they were given a room with two single beds. There was no way that they were going to sleep in single beds, so they would sleep in one of the beds and the next morning rumple up the other one very vigorously before they went down to breakfast. Then while they were at breakfast the servants would come up and make the beds for them. Somehow it seemed safer or perhaps more proper for the servants to believe that they had slept in separate beds.

Maybeth recalled her pessimism at the thought that she would live a single life in China, and prayed there in gratefulness to God for all that He had done. They had known each other for only a short time and yet were filled with absolute confidence that God had definitely brought them together. It seemed so perfect and there, while the war threatened on the threshold of China, they were content. The boy from the ranches of Alberta and the missionary's kid from China might have seemed an unlikely match, but God knew otherwise.

CHAPTER ELEVEN

Immediately after the honeymoon they headed down the coast south of Shanghai to their first Mission station together. The province of Zhejiang was the smallest province in China and one of the most productive. The delta of the Yangtze River provided rich soil and plentiful water. The countryside, however, was hilly and many of the fields were terraced so that rice could be grown and the water controlled. Small streams wended their way among the hillsides, which on occasion became raging torrents flooding the land nearby. In the south and west of the province the hills became more mountainous and less cultivated.

The Lord God had certainly "combined their ministries" Maybeth thought as Ken had suggested a year ago. They arrived in the lovely little city of Fenghua just south of Shanghai, famous as the birthplace of Chang Kai-Shek. Those first years at this Mission station were some of the happiest of their lives. Their house suited them perfectly. The two-story house stood in the middle of a good-sized garden with a wall all around it. A lawn graced the front of the house and a few tall trees sheltered the compound from the sun. Such a house and garden complex enclosed in a wall was referred to as a compound. Lawlessness was rampant in China and walls were used extensively to keep bandits out of the cities and out of a house. Fenghua, like Lienshui, was a walled city where the gates were closed at nightfall to protect the inhabitants from bandits who marauded in the country, but the house and grounds were also enclosed in a wall to protect from robbers within the city.

Ken Gray, almost as soon as he arrived in China had fallen in love with everything Chinese. He loved the Chinese people. He studied their history, admired their art, cherished their traditions, became fluent in their language, and learned to cook their food. His entire life was from that point on was influenced by his love of the Chinese. Long after leaving China, anything Chinese would draw his eye. The years in Fenghua confirmed that trait in him.

Maybeth and Ken loved their house in Fenghua because above all else they wanted a place where they could be on a similar social level with the people. They certainly did not want the biggest house in the city, thus appearing to be rich. Such an image would only hamper their ministry, so they were glad the house was small. They had wicker furniture and straw matting on the floor; all goods made locally. Of the houses missionaries lived in, many were so fancy that the Chinese didn't want to go into them. Maybeth and Ken wanted a house where people would feel at home and where they could come and stay overnight or stop for meals. One old blacksmith often visited them, coming into the house, sitting with his feet curled up on the chair, and saying, "I like it here with you."

They worked there out of that little house among a great variety of people, but try as they might, they still remained somewhat intimidating to the Chinese. One evening, they invited a Chinese Christian lady to stay for the night because she lived a good distance away, and it was getting late. Maybeth showed the lady guest to a room with the bed made up with sheets. Their guest had no idea what to do with the bed. She was quite embarrassed by it all. Quickly Maybeth learned to keep their customs as similar to the Chinese as possible. After that embarrassment, when they had Chinese staying the night they put a quilt on the bed--just the kind of quilt the Chinese use. Then their guests felt at home and curled up in the quilt just as they would at home.

The Christian work in the city was a work that Hudson Taylor had started. Hudson Taylor, the founder of the China Inland Mission, had taught the truth about God in that city in many unusual ways. One early story was that he brought a man to an understanding of his need of salvation from sin, and the man immediately went home into the country nearby and with great zeal went into a temple saying, "God's going to destroy this temple in three days. He will burn it down, so that you all will know that it is God who reigns above and not your idols."

After making this pronouncement, he realized that what he had said was rather scary and was frightened at his own words. He rushed back to Ningbo, where Hudson Taylor was staying, and said, "What am I going to do? I've told them that if God is real and alive, this temple is going to be burned down in three days." Hudson Taylor rebuked him and taught him that he should not make such pronouncements without clear direction from God. Such events were not our doing, Taylor told him. They were in the providence of God, but he added that he would be praying for him and that he was to go right back home to that area where the temple was. On the way back, the man saw huge clouds in the sky; the temple, struck by lightning, was totally destroyed. Such apparent miracles made a great impression on the people in the area.

Another account was about a man on a nearby country outstation, one where Maybeth and Ken worked later, who had a serious case of malaria and in his feverous state dreamed that an angel came to him and said, "Your malaria is serious: I have a remedy for you. There's a little herb that grows beside the big stones that make your doorstep. If you pull it out of the ground and cook it for a long time, and then drink the juice, this herb will cure your malaria. As soon as you're better and strong enough to walk, go to Ningbo, and when you get there look for a sign which reads "the Way of Life." The sick man didn't know the four characters making up that statement. However, when he cooked the weed and drank the juice, he got better. (Maybeth discovered that it later became a very common remedy for malaria).

Following the angel's instructions, he walked to Ningbo. When he got there, he stopped at a little teashop, similar to those that stand outside every large city, so people walking can sit down and have tea. These shops don't charge anything for tea; it's free tea for anyone walking past. As he walked into the teashop he saw many villagers sitting around discussing the news of the day. And then a strange white man, wearing Chinese clothes and a long pigtail, walked into the teashop. He asked permission to put up a poster on the wall. The proprietor agreed and this stranger hung up a big poster. To the watcher's surprise, on the top of the poster were those four characters -"the Way of Life." Then

Hudson Taylor spoke briefly about the meaning of those four characters on his sign to those who would listen. This man was so intrigued by the words that he followed Hudson Taylor back to his home in Ningbo and became a devout Christian. When he returned to the hills he started a church, teaching many people to trust in Christ.

It was many years later that missionaries coming into the area found an established church. The Christians had built a building and were worshipping God regularly, a direct result of the one man who had heard the message from Hudson Taylor.

With this kind of history, Maybeth and Ken felt very privileged to work in the church in the Fenghua area. . It was exciting to be working in a place where they could so readily see God's work in many unexpected ways, even in miracles that had been eye-openers to the Chinese people there. Ken was the pastor of eleven country churches and outreach programs where he led a Bible class or a small group in worship. He and Maybeth, riding their bicycles, traveled to remote and primitive churches in small nearby villages. Although they felt the shortage of workers and often became weary with the monumental task of pastoring such a widespread area, it was a wonderful three years. They enjoyed watching as God answered prayer and many grew in their faith and understood the Word of God better. Unfortunately the peace did not last and soon the rumblings of war began again.

The Chinese-Japanese war was well underway and within a few months of their arrival in Fenghua, news came that the Japanese were driving from the coast into the interior where Ken and Maybeth were, a little bit west and south of Shanghai.

As expected, prior to invasion, the Japanese started bombing. The area near the city was bombed continually that summer of 1939. The bombing continued and remained constant because this was Chang Kai-Shek's hometown, and he was the focal point of Japanese hatred. On the side of a hill in the town was a huge white building which housed a library which, Maybeth understood, was either built in Chang Kai-Shek's honor or by his family. It was a huge building and a perfect target for Japanese bombs. Nearby there was a very beautiful cemetery with huge headstones that designated the future burial places of Chang Kai-Shek and his family.

Ken soon concluded that this building was serving as a training ground for the young pilots. The planes came in and slowly circled, often for hours, taking a good look at the city. Then they would dive bomb the library on the side of the hill. The targets were a little distance from Maybeth and Ken's little compound, and they could watch as the planes dived and bombed the library. Gradually, as the pilots would get more accurate, they would move to the tombstones as targets. Maybeth became so accustomed to this pattern that she never thought they would actually bomb the city. All the bombing was being done on these monuments outside the city.

One day, as she watched the planes circling, she noticed something coming down from one of them. It looked like a big shiny ball, and she called to Ken to show him. He took one look, grabbed her by the arm, and dragged her into the shelter. It was the first bomb they had seen in the city and Maybeth hadn't even realized what it was. The first wave of bombing in the city killed one of the Christian ladies in the church and Ken and Maybeth grieved as the reality of war struck home.

Her report in the CIM monthly newsletter, however, told of the strength of some of the Chinese Christians:

"And what did you do when the planes came?" The question was put to the wife of the evangelist the evening after the city had been bombed for the first time, and some of the Christians who had gathered together for a meeting were discussing the events of the day before. The woman questioned is a bright Christian who truly serves the Lord in her home and in bringing up a family of children who are learning to love God at an early age.

She smiled and answered. "My husband was away shopping on the street at the time, so I did not know what to do. But when my little girl started to cry, I called the children around me and we sat here by our door under this vine and sang a chorus together while planes flew overhead. We sang, 'I have a Savior who is mighty to keep...' We were not so afraid when we were singing like that!"

I marveled that she could lead her children in song at such a time. They have lusty voices and I have never heard them sing without seemingly almost bursting their lungs with the volume of sound – so perhaps for them the singing helped to drown out the sound of planes and bombing around them. We praise God for Christians like these who know how to really trust the Lord.

In part because of the uncertainty of the times and in part because they had nothing else, Ken and Maybeth decided that they would use their wedding gifts immediately. From the first week they lived in Fenghua, they used their best china and silverware. It was a great delight for Maybeth to see the table set so beautifully in the lovely blue china they had bought in Shanghai. They put the new sheets on their bed and used the lovely tablecloths given to them for wedding presents. They used all they had been given for wedding gifts every day and put nothing back for a later date. They did not know that they had only three years to use them and then would have to leave them behind.

CHAPTER TWELVE

Fear of Japanese invasion was uppermost in the minds of most of the citizens of Fenghua. Word had spread about the horrific treatment of the Chinese in Nanking in December of 1937. Hundreds of innocent civilians and Nationalist soldiers had been summarily beheaded with the swords of the Japanese, and women by the score had been brutally raped, beaten and then killed. Because Japan was not at war with the United States or Canada from 1939 to 1941, nationals of those countries were theoretically safe from Japanese reprisals. But the peace was a tenuous one, and nationals like Ken and Maybeth Gray, Canadian citizens, could only count on neutral status as long as the United States and Canada had not declared war on Japan.

Shortly after the first bombs fell in Fenghua, Maybeth discovered to her delight that she was pregnant. Morning sickness plagued her for weeks on end, and she lay on a bed that summer, feeling miserable. Finally, after some weeks, the nausea wore off and she felt better. The excited couple went down to Ningbo to have a check-up at the hospital there. There they met a fine young doctor, George Sgalitzer and his wife, Hannah. Dr. Sgalitzer, an Austrian Jew, had fled from Hitler's Germany to Switzerland and then to Shanghai. He was looking for work, and the American Baptist doctor in Ningbo was going home on furlough and had no one to take his place. He asked Dr. Sgalitzer to come and take over the hospital. Ken and Maybeth soon discovered that Dr. Sgalitzer and his wife were, as Maybeth labeled them, "perfect dears", and that Dr. Sgalitzer was a brilliant surgeon. They made arrangements to come into Ningbo to stay just around Christmas time until the baby was to be born in January. They went back home to Fenghua and Maybeth carried on as well as she could. Ken did most of the traveling then, and she stayed at home.

About that time they were given a junior missionary from Vancouver to stay and intern with them. His name was Art Barber, a fastidious, fussy young man. He was simply revolted by anything that was dirty or even slightly lacking in hygiene. Ken and Maybeth had a lot of fun teasing him. Ken and Maybeth had early resolved to live native. They felt that if they lived in a manner that implied a more important status than the Chinese around them, they were implicitly suggesting that their God only loved those who were of higher status. They believed that if the Chinese could live simply, so could they.

On one nightmare of a trip, they took Art to O Dze, an outstation some distance off in the hills. It was a quaint little village where a group of Christians had asked for a week of Bible study. Ken and Maybeth were delighted at their interest and agreed to come. They ate just what the locals ate and enjoyed the food, but they also knew Art's squeamishness about food. Packed in baskets on their bikes, they took a can of powdered cocoa and some powdered milk so that they could make hot chocolate. Maybeth baked a batch of homemade cookies also to take along. The plan was that Art could fill up on cookies and hot chocolate if he didn't like the food at any particular meal.

When they arrived at the village, they found that the Chinese Christians had arranged that Art would sleep in a room with several of the pastors from various distant stations. Their thought was that Art would have a good opportunity to learn Chinese there with them. Maybeth and Ken were assigned another room nearby. Poor Art! He couldn't sleep all night. The Chinese pastors all snored and Art couldn't sleep a wink. He tossed and turned on the straw mattress on the floor.

The next day Art told Ken that he had problems sleeping and eating and didn't know what to do. Ken went and talked to one of the Chinese pastors who had a house just a little distance off. He explained that Art couldn't sleep in the room with all the pastors. Their host was most accommodating and suggested that all three of them go and sleep in his house up on the hill. He suggested that they might all sleep better up there since it was quieter. That evening he took them up to the little house and there they found three bedrooms in a row. All three of them were to share the middle room.

There were two big beds in the room with curtains around them to keep out mosquitoes and, as it turned out, whatever else might bother one in the night. Ken and Maybeth settled down in one of the beds that first night and carefully tucked the curtains in under the mattress to protect against anything that crawled. Art slept in the other bed. What a night they had! The walls were very very thin. They were made of a rattan sort of material with thin plaster over the rattan. The plaster had developed holes from everyday use. In the adjoining bedroom on one side was a girl with whooping cough and she coughed and moaned all through the night. Whooping violently! In the bedroom on the other side was a fellow who was dying of TB and he also coughed violently. When he had a coughing spell, it sounded as though he would cough his entire insides out.

To add to Art's misery, rats ran around the room all night. They ran across the top of the canopy and up and down the curtains. Ken and Maybeth felt quite safe from them since it was a rare rat that would come through the mosquito netting that they had tucked under the mattress. Ken and Maybeth easily fell asleep with the consumptive cough on one side and the whooping cough on the other and the scurrying rats. They slept well, but not Art. By the time Ken and Maybeth got Art home to Fenghua, he was a nervous wreck.

Near Christmas time, 1939, Maybeth decided that they should head for Ningbo so that she would be there in time for the baby to be born. The Mission decided at that time to move Art to another Mission station. They traveled to Ningbo by boat on an overnight trip. On a bed in the bottom of the boat, the three of them all slept together Ken in the middle with Art on one side and Maybeth on the other. The blankets were no wider than the bottom of the boat, so as the chill of night descended, Art and Maybeth pulled and tugged the covers back and forth over Ken.

When they arrived at Ningbo, they were met by a young lady, Art's fiancée, who was stationed not far from the city. Imagine Maybeth's embarrassment when they got off the boat and Art and Annie Lee went into a bear hug on the dock. Showing affection openly was something that no one did in China at that time and Ken and Maybeth were embarrassed for Art and for the Chinese who politely looked the other way.

Art and Annie Lee eventually got married and went back to the USA. Chinese life was not nearly hygienic enough for them and they could not adjust. He took a pastorate in the U.S. and was a good pastor, but China wasn't the place for him. It was simply too dirty and, in his view, unhealthy.

CHAPTER THIRTEEN

Free of Art and Annie Lee, Ken and Maybeth stayed in Dr. Sgalitzer's home in Ningbo for almost a month. The baby was two weeks late by their reckoning. Ken and Maybeth took long walks every night and thoroughly enjoyed the company of the Sgalitzers. Long evenings of conversation about world affairs made for an enjoyable time.

As she labored to deliver her first child, she recalled Dr Sgalitzer, who was always very interested in the noon news on the radio, say, "Let's hurry this kid along. I need to hear the noon broadcast." Sure enough GwenEnid arrived before noon, January 25, 1940, a healthy little girl, 7lbs 10 oz. Ken and Maybeth stayed in Ningbo a couple weeks more before heading back with her to Fenghua. They didn't see the Sgalitzers again in China.

There was great excitement, of course, among the Christians to have a missionary baby in the city. Of course, Ken and Maybeth were thrilled and the Chinese excitement added to that delight. They made beautifully embroidered shoes, the customary gift for newborns. Gwen wore a different pair of shoes every single Sunday for church. She was the joy of their hearts. The Chinese neighbors would all come in to see her and the children to play with her.

As spring in 1940 arrived and the weather became warm, the Japanese again made inroads into China. Bombing began again in earnest and it was a rare day when Japanese bombers did not fly over Fenghua. In their compound on the edge of town, Ken made a makeshift bomb shelter. When air raid signals began, he and his little family headed for a dugout in the corner of the garden. It was really a smokehouse where Ken had smoked sausages, but he had made it into a shelter, knowing that the house was not strong enough to withstand bombing near it. When Ken had made sausages in that dugout, he had put sandbags all around it and burned sawdust for a slow fire in it, but now that there was war, it made a safe retreat from the shrapnel that was likely to land in the compound. Ken and Maybeth knew that it was not protection from a direct hit, but so often they had seen Chinese killed by the debris of metal and wood that flew after a bomb hit the ground.

Meanwhile the alarm system was in place. The air raid alarms were the huge temple bells. At first when there was news of a possible attack, the bells would sound slowly: ding- dong, ding-dong, ding-dong, and then, as the planes got closer, they would sound faster, and finally when the news came that the city was in the path of the bombers, they would ring very fast: ding-ding-ding-ding-ding-ding. Everybody then knew where the planes were. So Ken and Maybeth and little Gwen got used to rushing out to the shelter. The bombing continued daily until finally the Japanese drove in toward Fenghua and Maybeth and Ken wondered what would happen to them. As yet, before Pearl Harbor, America and Canada had not entered World War II. Fearful that they might be cut off from food or confined to their compound in the event of a Japanese takeover, they made preparations.

City officials and Mission leaders were told that if the Japanese came into the city, American and Canadian Missionaries didn't need to be afraid. Since they were neutral parties, the Japanese had said that they would not be harmed. But the word of the Japanese was not something Maybeth and Ken wanted to rely upon, so they made their own plans. As long as summer lasted food from the garden was plentiful and they had a female goat who was expecting, so milk would soon be available. Ken removed a board at the top of a line of studs in the wall, cleaned out what little insulation might have been in it and filled the space with rice. He then drilled a hole near the bottom of the wall and plugged it with a cork. That supply of rice did indeed stand them in good stead almost a year later. They tried to make 1940 as normal as possible, and yet, in the back of their heads, they knew that anything could happen.

The United States had sent money to assist the Chinese and there had been bombings of American ships on the Yangtze, but always the

Japanese would send an apology and claim accidental hits.

When Gwen was just over a year old and running around as beautiful as a child could be, in the spring of 1941, the Japanese drove toward Fenghua, and it wasn't long before they were right outside the city. Ken and Maybeth's compound wall was the city limit and just beyond their wall were fields. The Japanese came toward them from the north and the Chinese set up a defense of sorts in the city of Fenghua. Machine guns shot back and forth until the Chinese began to retreat into the fields behind them and the Japanese came into the city. In the interim, the two forces were lobbing shells back and forth over the top of Ken and Maybeth's small house. Their little "Mission matchbox" was caught in the middle with shells flying over the house and garden both ways. What a frightening day it was! Yet, the house and the family, spending most of their day in the bomb shelter, came to no harm.

When the Chinese Nationalist Army retreated, withdrawing from Fenghua, the entire city waited for the Japanese, not knowing what would happen to them. The Japanese bombed first, and then the army marched into the city, sending many of the Chinese fleeing before them out into the country. There were very few staying in their homes. They were too frightened to stay. Rumors were rampant. Stories from the massacre at Nanking were still fresh in their minds, and the people fled to avoid such a scene. As the army came into the city, the officers threw a hand grenade in every door. Ken didn't want the door of his house broken down, so he went out to the gate to meet the soldiers. They came into the little walled compound, surprised to find there were foreigners there and an officer asked who was in the house. Ken told him that there were very few people in the house; it was a very small house. The officer insisted that everyone that he had in the house be brought out and lined up so he could see "who the foreigner had in his house."

Knowing the reputation of the invading army in these circumstances, Ken and Maybeth had earlier invited the girls of the church and their cook and his wife to come and stay at the house when they knew the army was approaching the city. Maybeth put them all in the two tiny upstairs bedrooms. She also invited the pastor and his wife and little children to come and live upstairs, while she and Ken and little Gwen lived downstairs in the living room/ dining room.

The officer insisted on lining everyone in the house up in a long row and asking for their names. Then he stood there in the yard and studied the group. And then he left. Maybeth and Ken were grateful that they had no problem with him and assumed that their neutral status would ensure safety for themselves and the people they had invited in.

After the majority of the troops had gone by, Ken and Maybeth went over to the church and found the Japanese troops were stabling their horses in the church. They had thrown the benches all to one side and brought their horses in and were using one end of the church for a toilet. Ken protested. "God's house should not be used like this," he said. Amazingly, the commanders listened to him and slowly began to remove the troops, leaving Ken and Maybeth to shovel out all the filth. As they were working, a young Japanese soldier came along who spoke a little English. He was the first one they had met who spoke any English. He told them that he had been taught English in a Mission school in Japan. He told them that he understood about Christianity from his schooling. He was a little apologetic about the way the soldiers had made use of the church. Ken and Maybeth were touched at his concern and interest in them.

No sooner had Ken and Maybeth cleaned up some of the worst of the mess at the church than they heard that there were soldiers in their house using their well and trampling in the garden and using the house as though it were their own. They rushed back to the house and Ken asked that they honor the fact that he and his family were neutral and not trespass.

Ken then went to the officer in charge of the occupation of the city and explained to him that he did not want soldiers to enter the compound, and that, since he and his family were third party nationals, it was their right. The officer agreed with him and gave him a seal to put on the door of the compound which proclaimed that those who lived there were neutral parties and that no Japanese soldier was to enter the compound. With relief they posted the sign with the seal of the commanding officer sure that they would be left alone and secure. They all went to bed that night feeling relieved and confident that the worst was over and now they would be protected.

That night, soon after midnight, there was a terrible banging at the door. Ken went out and two Japanese soldiers, an officer and a common soldier, came in with him. Maybeth looked around the corner from the back room and realized that it was the same officer who had given him the proclamation earlier that evening -- dead drunk and very wild looking and accompanied by the young soldier who had spoken to them in the church. He said, through the young man who served as interpreter, "I want a girl from here tonight. I want one of your women."

Ken bravely said, "No, we don't do that. We're Christians; we don't allow that."

And the officer said, "Oh, but you do for me." And he sat down at the dining room table.

Maybeth could hear everything that was said. In terror she held Gwen tightly and prayed for safety for Ken as he confronted this evil man. Because the young officer was limited in his English, Ken and the officer conversed mostly by writing in Chinese characters because the Chinese characters and Japanese characters are similar. The spoken word was very dissimilar, but the written offered a way to communicate.

As the officer sat down beside Ken, he drew a long sword from a sheath at his side and said, "This is what you'll get if you don't produce a woman right away for me."

Maybeth clutched her baby to her breast and strained to hear as much of the conversation as she could. She was terrified as she heard what Ken was saying, and it was not hard to gather what was going on. The officer took the sword and picked up some pencils off the table, sharpening them with the blade. It was razor sharp.

He repeated his threat. "You will feel that – your head will be off, if you don't give me a woman immediately."

What could they do? Maybeth strained to hear and trembled as the time passed. Her mind raced with fears of living in Japanese-occupied China without Ken's protection. She tried to pray but no words came to her mind. She could see Ken's hands shaking as he wrote down his end of the conversation.

Everyone in the house was motionless, too scared to pray, shaking. The only sound was the officer making shavings of the pencils. The women upstairs knew that no good could come of the officer in the house at midnight, but they were less aware of what was going on.

Finally Ken repeated, "No, we cannot do that. We're Christians; we don't allow that."

The officer argued. "I know you have these people. Bring one down from upstairs."

Ken kept refusing and the officer kept threatening him with the sword. Then the officer put the sword back in the sheath and took out Chinese coins, silver coins, which were the best currency at the time, and started to pile them up higher and higher, offering to give Ken all of it if he'd bring him one woman.

"No, I don't want any of your money."

Right beside him was the young Japanese common soldier listening and interpreting. Suddenly he nudged the officer with his elbow and said, "Let's go somewhere else."

Abruptly and with no apparent reason, the officer stood up and he and the young man walked out of the house. As he walked out, the officer took a piece of paper and sealed the door of the compound with the announcement that no one was allowed to leave this place without his permission. "Nobody may go in or out of this place until I give permission," he barked.

Ken stood with relief and the women listening upstairs came downstairs. They fell to their knees and offered a heartfelt prayer of thanksgiving as the officers left the compound.

It was about three weeks before he took the seal off the door, allowing them to leave the compound. Meanwhile the little group in the compound had rice from the wall in the living room and some vegetables in the garden. They had the goat for milk for Gwen. The goat had three kids which ensured a good supply of fresh milk, and Ken slaughtered one of the kids for meat.

One day as Maybeth was in the garden a bundle came hurtling over the stone wall that surrounded the compound. In it was a bag full of peas in their pods and other vegetables. On succeeding days the packages would continue to fall, always with extra food. It was literally like the Biblical story of Elijah being fed in the wilderness by ravens. The Christians in the town were supplying more food than those behind the compound wall needed. They had the necessities, rice and vegetables, but their friends kept giving extras out of the kindness of their hearts. It was dangerous for them to be helping the family, but their love for Ken and Maybeth and the others confined in that compound made them bold enough to take the risk.

That was in 1941. Five years later when Ken and Maybeth came home on furlough, after the war, they met various prayer partners and friends. One prayer partner of Ken's in Calgary, Lem Fowler, had a story to tell them. Lem, the friend who had sent the money for Ken to buy Maybeth an engagement ring, was a great friend of Ken's father and they often met for lunch. One day Lem and Ken's father met in Calgary, Alberta, in a coffee shop for lunch. Part way through the meal, Lem turned to Ken's dad and said, "I am anxious about Ken and Maybeth. I don't know what it is, but I feel we must pray for them."

So they sat in a corner of the coffee shop as far away as possible from the people that were coming and going and prayed together for Ken and Maybeth. They said, "Lord, we don't know what is happening to them. We haven't heard from them for weeks and weeks. The mail seems to be stopped because of the war conditions. But Lord, whatever the situation in their place right now – please protect them and keep them." And they prayed earnestly together in spite of people going back and forth and laughing and talking in the coffee shop. They prayed that God would protect their loved ones so far away in war-torn China.

Ken asked them for the time frame and Lem told him that he had written down the date afterwards because he wanted to check it out with Ken. They compared the time and it was the very moment that Ken and Maybeth and the Chinese in their home had been so threatened by the Japanese officer. It had been noon in Calgary, but midnight in China.

Maybeth learned a lesson in faith that lasted her for the rest of her life. She believed that prayer of this kind at the moment it is needed happens often, and she believed it would happen more often if believers kept in tune with God and realized that there are often times when friends, no matter what country they are in, might be in real danger or severely tempted by the Devil in some way and God gently reminds them. If believers are in tune with Him, God will tell them to pray for someone in need and they may never learn what the situation was –never know how that prayer was answered. Maybeth, late in her life said that she was "convinced that when we get to glory we will hear some of these things – things that we hadn't heard here on earth – people who had been faithful in prayer, prayer that God answered. I am certainly sure that happened many times in China. So many people were so faithful in praying for us, often having no idea how dangerous the situation was or how difficult the situation was. God hears."

CHAPTER FOURTEEN

Sometime after those three weeks, the climate in the town settled down somewhat. The house arrest was lifted and Maybeth and Ken and those living with them in the little house could come and go as they pleased. A mayor, who was really just a puppet for the Japanese, was appointed. He was a local man who had been educated in Japan and could speak Japanese. He was also a Christian; Maybeth believed that he had taken the position so that he would be able to help protect his own people from some of the ravages of war.

Ken and Maybeth as Canadians were designated as third party nationals. The Chinese were fighting the Japanese, but neutral parties were supposed to be guaranteed safety and normal living conditions during the war. International law protected such people at times like this. After the incident with the Japanese officer who threatened Ken's life, the guarantee lost its credibility. It was hard to know what to do. They kept as much as possible out of the way of the officers involved.

Sometimes Japanese officers and soldiers came to the compound and were very friendly. They were charmed with Gwen and played with her or brought her a little basket of oranges or other fruit. Every day, however, a foreboding sense of danger intruded on the family. Ken particularly knew that it was probably inevitable that Canada or the United States would become involved in the war sweeping the world. As soon as that happened, he knew, he and Maybeth would be the enemy and no longer neutral parties. As the enemy, they would be in danger of being treated as hundreds of others, Chinese and European alike, had been treated, with cruelty and inhumanity. Stories had come to them from other provinces relating how Chinese civilians had been murdered and tortured, and he knew that they would be treated no better and probably worse.

Every day planes flew overhead – more than twenty planes going south. Wondering what the big picture was, they wrote to Mission headquarters. Suspicious of foreigner's mail, Japanese soldiers censored all correspondence before it left the post office, but the CIM had created a code, a relatively complicated one, in a thick codebook. This codebook wasn't exactly secret; all the missionaries knew it, but it made it handy for sending telegrams – a whole sentence could be summed up in a ten-letter word. Ken and Maybeth's letters inquiring about the state of travel and asking for instructions went something like this, "Now we have friends in Africa who like to go fishing in (and they would use a code word for the name of the city where they were thinking about moving).

The Mission authorities would write back. "They get interesting (codeword) fish there."

Correspondence back and forth with the Mission headquarters in Shanghai using these code words was quite exciting and although they knew the danger, they felt like secret agents. Japanese censors didn't know one fish from another or for that matter one city from another. In the process of sending code messages to the Mission, Ken asked permission, in the event of war breaking out between Japan and Canada, to escape the city. The Mission leaders wrote back and said that he should do whatever God wanted him to do, including escape if that was most expedient. The Mission leaders knew that Ken's proximity to the problem made him the one to make those kinds of decisions. So Ken and Maybeth made plans to get out of that Japanese occupied area if they had a chance and a suitable occasion arose.

The Japanese army was driving westward and south from Shanghai, and in 1941 Fenghua was right on the border of free China and occupied China. There were a few scares as their plans were almost exposed. Ken had been surreptitiously sending coded messages back and forth to the Mission headquarters, where prayer was offered for them. One missionary wrote very naively, never thinking of censorship saying, "I hear you folks are planning to escape into Free China. We are too. What are your plans?" This letter apparently went through the censorship. Maybeth and Ken's hearts sank as they saw the letter and for a few days they lived in fear that their escape plans would be exposed to the Japanese authorities. Nothing came of that letter, but Ken and Maybeth heard that that couple was caught later and suffered in an interment camp for several years. Fortunately for Ken and Maybeth, the Japanese censors did not connect the discussion with them. Again God intervened and they were safe from human error and naiveté.

In the light of discussions with the Mission leaders and what they were able to hear about world news, Ken and Maybeth planned their escape to free China. As soon as they heard that Japan was at war with Canada, they would try to escape across a no-man's land, which was a stretch of about thirty or forty miles. They talked about it a little bit and made getaway plans.

Meanwhile Ken would go outside the city gates every day to buy vegetables and sometimes to teach and preach in the villages in the country, and Maybeth would stay at home with Gwen. She would do what teaching she could in the church, and they did their best to carry on as usual. The Japanese had not pushed further west into China. They had stayed in the city of Fenghua and had not moved any further in over six months. Ken presumed they were consolidating their gains and preparing to continue west later. Fenghua was right on the edge of neutral territory between the Japanese and the Chinese Nationalist troops. Actually the Chinese had done a great deal of destruction to the infrastructure in attempts to curb the advance of the Japanese troops. They had blown up railways and roads and broken up supply trains to prevent or slow down the advancing Japanese. But now, under Chiang-Kai-Shek, they appeared to be marking time until the Americans would enter the war. They believed America's entrance into the war was their only real hope against a far better equipped and trained Japanese army.

After trying to get world news from newspapers that were seldom delivered or from the rumors of the Chinese, which were almost always exaggerated, Ken decided that he needed a more reliable source of information. With the help of a Christian friend, Ken made a radio that they kept in their living room; actually it was just a tiny crystal set with earphones. Periodically the Japanese would come and check on this radio in their normal round of inspections of the house. They were always interested to see what the foreigners were listening to. Ken always had it tuned to Tokyo so they thought that was the only station he could get. But Ken listened to Manila twice a day at seven in the morning and seven at night. He had to do some adjustments to the aerial on the crystal set to get Manila, but he faithfully listened to the BBC news twice a day. It wasn't long before the listening proved vitally important.

PART THREE – FLIGHT

"When through the deep waters, I call you to go,
The rivers of sorrow shall not overflow.
For I will be with you your troubles to bless
And sanctify to you your deepest distress."

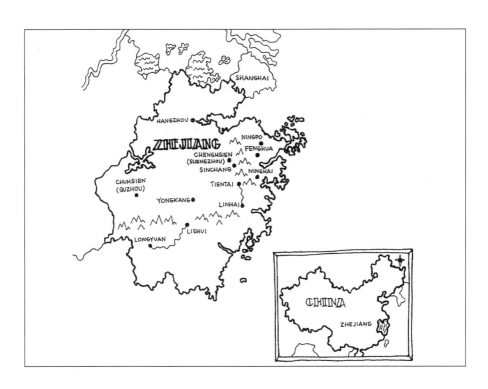

Zhejiang province, also called Chekiang in 1940.

CHAPTER FIFTEEN

Every day they had expected it, but still it came as a surprise. It was December 8, 1941. The Japanese had bombed Pearl Harbor and the US and Canada had declared war on Japan. Ken and Maybeth were tired and had slept in an extra fifteen minutes, and were groggily beginning their morning routine when Ken heard the news stutter bluntly over the broken airwaves. No amount of expectation had prepared them. The advancing Japanese troops notoriously took few prisoners, and now they were looking for any opportunity to show their contempt of the West. Ken and Maybeth had to escape, and had to escape now. It was 7:15 am.

Ken rushed to the first floor with the news and without further words being spoken they both knew what needed to be done. Quickly changing out of their nightclothes, they put on as many of their winter clothes as possible. Gwen, not quite two years old at the time, was quickly awakened and bundled up. Making snap decisions they collected only the most essential items - a couple of changes of clothes, some official papers, their Bibles, and Ken's beloved hymnbook - and loaded them into the two wicker panniers on the back of their bikes. In twenty minutes they were out of the house. Time didn't allow them to think about their predicament or even to pray.

Awkward with the many layers of heavy clothing, they set off, Gwen seated on the crossbar seat of Ken's battered old bike. As they approached the city gates, they saw the Japanese guards who lolled around the check-points. What normally seemed benign, in the light of Pearl Harbor filled them with apprehension. Did the guards know these two Canadians were now enemies? With unknown wisdom Ken had ridden through the gates several mornings each week to go out into the country to buy vegetables. So looking as natural as possible, Ken waved as he approached the gate, his smile tight with fear. Accustomed as they were to seeing Ken each morning, the guards simply waved back and signaled the couple through. As the guards' attention flicked back to a Chinese man trying to exit the city, Ken and Maybeth instinctively sped up, desperate to put as much distance between them and the Japanese guards as possible.

Immediately upon leaving the city, they were in no-man's land – controlled neither by the Japanese nor the Chinese Nationalist Army. They pedaled south along the country roads, trying to take as straight a path as they could towards Free China. Ken's frequent trips to the outlying villages proved invaluable as he led his family along the back-roads– bumpy and potholed, sometimes taking shortcuts on footpaths through paddy fields. Always he tried to stay hidden from any Japanese army jeeps that may have been traveling through.

The day wore on to a hot noon. The sun glared down on their backs and sweat soaked their many layers of clothing. Eyes hazy with heat and exhaustion, Maybeth did not see the old gentleman step out into the path, staring at the spectacle of their white skin, as they darted past on their bikes. She swerved into the undergrowth, twigs and scrub snagging at her clothes and skin, till she hit a tree root and toppled from her seat. The front wheel of her ancient bike was bent in half. Their only hope of escape was now damaged beyond repair. Unmoved by the accident, the man simply continued to stare.

Fear struck her heart again as she realized their precarious predica-ment. Here they were, as their only transportation, a bike with a wheel that wouldn't even go around and the three of them trying to get away with their lives.

Thinking quickly, Ken realized that they were near the home of a Chinese man he knew. His knowledge of the people in the area included many Christians in remote villages and one right in this area. Ken took the bike into the home of the Christian, who had heard the news of the bombing of Pearl Harbor, and, immediately understanding the predica-ment they were in, offered to get a rickshaw right away. He suggested that the baby and Maybeth ride in the rickshaw and Ken ride the bicycle alongside. Without telling the rickshaw man what they were doing, the Good Samaritan simply told him to run as fast as he could down to the next city. "Go as fast as you can possibly go," he said. "The faster you go the more they'll pay you for it."

Maybeth rode in the rickshaw with Gwen and Ken rode alongside. Ken knew that they had already lost time and so he set a pace that the rickshaw driver struggled to meet. The day wore on and traffic increased on the roads. Maybeth sat in the rickshaw looking straight ahead and praying as they traveled. Sometimes people would come quickly up behind them and Maybeth, now that the exertion of pedaling the bicycle was gone, had time to think. She became almost paralyzed with fear. Perhaps the people coming up from behind were Japanese soldiers chasing them, she thought. She was terrified all day. Several times during the day, she saw Japanese soldiers in the distance and wondered if they were coming out to forage food from the locals as they often did, or if they were coming out of the city to catch Ken and her and the baby.

They traveled on as quickly as possible all that day – very frightened. The Japanese foraging parties continued driving through that area taking food from the farmers and they expected that at any moment they might be stopped.

They wondered why the news wasn't out yet. Before the attack on Pearl Harbor there had existed an uneasy lull in the fighting in China. Ken and Maybeth knew the habits of the Japanese occupying forces in Fenghua and knew that they played mah-jongg, a gambling game, until late into the night. Then because there was no immediate fighting those days, they would wake up late and have a late breakfast. Maybeth presumed that was the reason they had not heard the news before Ken did. The early morning broadcast had been their salvation. At any time, they thought, the Japanese would hear the news that Canada and the USA had declared war and chase after them. As the day wore on they became more frightened knowing that the Japanese must know about Pearl Harbor by that time. Drawing nearer and nearer to an area that was not occupied by the Japanese, they kept up a constant prayer for safety to the Godwho had brought them to China. He had already proved Himself faithful in the last few months especially, and although frightened, they knew they were in the hands of Almighty God.

Two days passed in the same manner, with little sleep or food and terror gripping their hearts. They stayed in the home of another Chinese Christianfriend the first night and for the next day because heavy rain prevented their further flight. Gwen played happily with the Chinesechildren and Kenand Maybeth kept as low a profile as they could. They arrived the following night in Ninghai, where they knew there was a church to welcome them. Exhausted mentally and physically, they pushed themselves to make the city. They arrived quite late, relieved to be among Chinese soldiers, occupying free China. Ken told the soldiers about Pearl Harbor and that war had been declared by the Americans and Canadians. The soldiers threw their hands in the air, delighted beyond measure with the news which they had not yet heard, communication being very poor among the troops. This was the news they had waited to hear and they were elated. Ken and Maybeth watched the soldiers rejoice and did their own rejoicing, having reached what they thought was comparative safety. The days had been long and their fear was only beginning to subside as they arranged for a place to spend that night.

Back in their home city of Fenghua, no more than a half an hour after Ken and Maybeth left their house that morning, Japanese soldiers came to look for them to take them prisoner but couldn't find them. They searched the city. The officer in charge in the city had lost face because he had been responsible for only two foreigners and he had let them escape.

Their actions were no surprise to Ken and Maybeth. They had known that if the Japanese suddenly viewed them as the enemy, in the event of a declaration of war, they would have no chance. It was one thing in the larger cities to be neutral, but they had already had the experience of the Japanese officer demanding a woman in their house. They knew that any peace they had with the Japanese army was very tenuous and that it could be violated at any time. In these small backwoods cities, the danger was great since news seldom leaked out to authorities. If they had stayed, they were sure to be killed eventually and perhaps, in the meantime, held up to ridicule by the Japanese.

The Japanese soldiers captured Boh Jing, the Gray's faithful friend and cook and his wife. An officer came to the compound and wanted to know where the foreigners had gone. Boh Jing said that he didn't know. Ken and Maybeth had purposely not told him where they were going, in the vain hope that perhaps he would be believed and not tortured. But later that day, the Japanese officers caught up with him at his house and beat him to within an inch of his life because he couldn't tell them what had happened to Ken and Maybeth. Then the soldiers insisted that he tell them where the Grays had hidden any of their belongings. After taking terrible abuse at the hands of the soldiers, Boh Jing finally told them the name of the lady who had stored their boxes of belongings. He felt terrible that he had perhaps implicated the Christian lady and also that they would destroy all the Gray's belongings. The soldiers immediately went to the house and took inventory of the boxes. There were five boxes, three of them trunks and two of them boxes of canning jars, a precious commodity in inland China at the time. The officer saw the three trunks and didn't notice the boxes of canning jars. They told the lady of the house that the three trunks of the missionaries were to be left right there and that they would come back later and pick them up. In the meantime she was not to touch them.

Before the soldiers came back to pick up the trunks, the lady of the house had filled two of the trunks with canning jars and had hidden the other boxes. When the soldiers came later that week, they took one box of belongings and two trunks of canning jars. Years later when Ken returned to Fenghua, the lady gave him back those two boxes. There were some items in those boxes that were very precious: items belonging to Ken's father and a typewriter.

As Ken and Maybeth bicycled across the back roads, they were sure they had left behind all their belongings forever: all their wedding gifts and many personal keepsakes. In later years when some of their belongings were returned, they were so grateful to a brave lady who dared to substitute canning jars for keepsakes.

The Grays met Boh Jing years later and he told them the story. He was still faithful to God and loyal to them. He simply loved them, harboring no hard feelings at all about what had happened that day. Maybeth grieved that he had suffered for their sakes, but his joy at seeing them again was unmistakable and he held no grudge.

CHAPTER SIXTEEN

When Ken and Maybeth reached Ninghai on December 10, they arrived to the welcome of the Christians there and to an empty home, the home of a missionary who had gone home on furlough. They moved in, so thankful to have a place to stay. The next morning they had bad news from one of the Christians back in Fenghua, who had run most of the night to bring it. He told them that the Japanese officer had angrily declared that if he could catch the foreigners, he'd kill them. He had lost face over letting them escape. The messenger pleaded, "Don't stay here. Go further away. It's not safe here."

Later that day they heard from Ken's friend Jack Sharman that they should come to Chenghsien and stay with them. He also told Ken that the British ships the H.M.S. Prince of Wales and the H.M.S. Repulse had been sunk by the Japanese. "What a blow!" Ken replied, understanding what war between Japan and Britain meant to his own family.

Even though they were in Free China, their situation was still precarious. With the insistent invitation of the Sharmans and with the arrival of two suspicious looking Chinese who nosed around their compound, they decided that it was time to leave. It was not uncommon for the Japanese to pay Chinese to spy in Free China and if those men informed the Japanese of where they were they could easily be taken captive.

Heeding the advice of the friend from Fenghua, Ken, Maybeth and little Gwen started out several days later for the city of Chenghsien, where their dear friends, Jack and Peggy Sharman, lived.

It was more than 45 miles to the west over a steep mountain road. The trip promised to be tough. Bandits had become bolder because of the upheaval in the war and the area through which the road wound was heavily populated with them. Ken and Maybeth, however, knew that it was the only reasonable plan because it meant that they would have a ready welcome and friends with whom to confer about the future. They also assumed that Chenghsien was far enough west of the Japanese army that they could work in safety there with their great friends, the Sharmans. Who knew? Perhaps the Americans would enter the war in China as the Nationalist Army hoped and they could soon return to Fenghua.

Ken had worked in Chenghsien with Jack before he was married, serving the church there for a year. It had been Ken's first year in China, and the Welshman had made Ken feel at home. Though they were from different continents and different backgrounds, Ken, the boy from the Canadian prairies, and Jack, a boy from the mining towns in Wales, they had quickly become fast friends. When Jack married Peggy in 1938, Ken had been his best man. Surely, Ken thought, they would find safety and good advice with the Sharmans.

The Christians in the Ninghai church paid for a sedan chair-- a chair carried by two men on two long poles on the shoulders, a man at one end, a man at the other end, and the chair on bamboo poles between-- to carry Gwen and Maybeth, as well as two men to carry their belongings. Although they had left Fenghua in a hurry and taken almost nothing with them, they had gathered a few necessities at the home where they stayed in Ninghai and some of the Chinese families had given them necessary items along the way, necessities like quilts and a change of clothes.

They started out early the morning of December 19, encouraged by the loving goodbyes of the Christians in Ninghai, people they had not known until the previous week, but a true family who promised to pray for their safety on their way. Ken wrote of the trip,

The country is lovely, and after some 10 miles, we got right into the mountains again. The winter air was not very cold, and the trip was more like a pleasure jaunt than a flight. After about 12 miles of easy traveling, we started climbing up the long mountain pass. Up and up we went in what seemed to us to be a road that 'wound up hill all the way, yes, to the very top.' As we went further up, the road clung to the side of the mountains and crossed and recrossed the rushing mountain stream on stone arched bridges covered with the moss of decades. Up and still up we went, climbing slowly, for it is hard going, and pushing a bike up hills like this is no joke, I assure you. We passed villages away up there in the hills with lots of underfed dogs which, of course, informed the neighbourhood of our coming. The villages up there make paper for a living, and load after load of paper met us on the way down to the larger towns and cities for market. We passed deep pits where the bamboo is soaking till it becomes soft enough to beat up into pulp from which they make the paper.

Then another thing which we enjoyed up in the hills was the number of little water-mills which hammered away and beat or ground for the people. Every village has lots of these mills nestled down in quiet corners of the river.

Finally after going up for some 7 more miles, we arrived at the bottom of a very long flight of steps. It seemed to us that we would never get up that long flight of stairs. Maybeth would go about ten steps and then rest for a while. I pushed and carried my bike up and up and up those never- ending stairs. Gwen rode in the chair like a little queen, munching on a sponge cake and as happy as a lark! Finally we reached the top, and sat down for an hour or so to wait till the carriers caught up. One of them was very slow, and all day long we had been fretting about the slowness which of course kept us all back as we could not afford to get separated too far."

The carriers had come with recommendations and seemed reliable, however, there were many times when they would be well behind and out of sight of Ken and Maybeth. Maybeth preferred to walk most of the way since Ken was walking, and the swaying motion of the sedan chair reminded her of a ship, causing the old seasickness to rise in her throat. Now and again gunshots would ring out in the valleys in the mountains, causing their hearts to pound and Ken wondered how near the bandits were.

As they walked and rode that day, fearful of the dangers in the valleys through which they passed, Ken and Maybeth prayed often for protection from evil. Evil seemed to be everywhere and although they were not in Japanese- occupied China there was no lack of frightening scenes. However, they were confident of the prayers of the people back in the church in Ninghai, and had not God delivered them on this perilous journey?

The slow carrier was surly and sullen. Ken tried to joke with him, talk to him and be pleasant with him, but found him very unresponsive. Not easily deterred, Ken continued to talk with him, offer to help him, and speak kindly to him.

They walked a long way that day and into the night hoping to put plenty of distance between their little party and the Japanese. That night they had no preplanned place to stop and sleep. It was getting close to evening and, tired beyond belief, they went into what the Chinese call a "lulong", a roadhouse, a small pole and thatched roof house by the side of the road. In these houses it was usually possible to get a free cup of hot tea. Those that hosted the travelers offered tea to strangers as a good deed to gain them merit in heaven.

As Ken and Maybeth with Gwen and the carriers wearily sat down to drink that welcome cup of tea, an old man came in from the opposite direction and sat down near them. Maybeth wondered why this old man was studying them so intently. Suddenly he turned to Ken and said "Reverend Gray, what are you doing here?" Maybeth looked fearfully at Ken wondering who this old man could be and if his recognition would mean that they would have to run for their lives.

Ken immediately recognized him, however, as an old friend, an itinerant preacher who often helped Ken with meetings in the countryside when he had been stationed in Chenghsien. Ken told him of their long journey that day and of their uncertainty where they would spend the night. He also told him in quiet tones of the difficulty they would face if the Japanese found them.

"Ah, you've come to the right place," he said and explained that this roadside inn was owned by Christians and there were a few rooms upstairs where he usually held services on Sunday mornings. This kind Chinese pastor took them upstairs and introduced them to the couple who owned the teahouse and they welcomed them all for the night. There was no question as to who they were or how much it would cost; the simple fact was that here were people in need and Christians help Christians. The carriers and the coolies were welcome also. A stack of straw, not terribly clean, served as a mattress for everyone: Ken, Maybeth, Gwen, the carriers and the coolies. They made themselves comfortable and Ken chatted with the carriers and coolies a little as night fell. As exhausted as they all were, sleep came quickly.

The next morning they were on the road again quickly and hoping to put many miles between them and the Japanese by nightfall. It was still uphill most of the way, and gunshots rang out frequently from the hills around. They knew the gunshots probably meant bandits in the hills. While China was at war, bandits had almost free reign, since the regular authorities were busy with the war effort. Ken tried to avoid paths where he thought the bandits would be. The coolies and chairmen were frightened at times of the possibility of being attacked by bandits. They never knew if they would simply take all their belongings or if they would shoot one or all of them in the process. There were frequent reports of bandit killings. Ken described the trip,

The next morning was wet and drizzly, but there was nothing for it but to start off for Singchang, which was over 30 miles away. Thirty miles is not such a great distance when you are on a good road, but over these country roads, and up and down the hills that we had to traverse, it is a good day's journey. We came to one pass on that mountainous road that was called "a little hill", but it seemed a lot more than that to us. I was feeling the effect of the previous day's travel in my legs, and they quite refused to carry the bike and me too up this 'little hill'. So Maybeth took a cord that I had, and, fastening it to the front of the bike, went ahead and helped by pulling. Gwen, of course, could travel in the chair, which was a blessing. Arriving at the top of the little hill, we went for many miles over red clay hills, up and down in a steady roll. Stands by the side of the road here and there served cooked sweet potatoes which never tasted quite as good as that day. We did go for them and it was a good cheap form of food, which was at the same time very satisfying. As we went on into the day, it got wetter and wetter. Not a real rain, but just a steady drizzle which made the clay slippery so that to cycle was almost impossible with the exception of very level places. The carriers were slipping all over the place and so the only thing for Maybeth to do was to walk.

About 3 p.m. we hit the old motor road, and from there on things were different. It was a small section of the road which had not been destroyed seriously, and so we could easily cycle along it at a good pace...Just as the winter sun was setting, we arrived in Singchang and traveled through the charred remains of that city to the undamaged chapel where we were warmly received by a Christian doctor who put us up for the night.

"What road did you come by?" asked Dr. Yu. and when we told him he exclaimed, "I can tell you now that you are over it, that you have come through the most dangerous bandit country, but God has cared for you and protected you from harm." Then, of course, our hearts went out all the more to God in praise for the wonderful way in which he had cared for us and kept us from harm on that two-day trek over the wild mountain district of Ninghai and Singchang.

Dr. Yu gave us good warm Chinese food which did taste good after our improvised meals on the trip. Warm water to wash in, and a good clean bed to sleep in; my but it felt so good! He has been bombed out completely having only a little store of drugs and medicines left with which to work. His home and his hospital were completely destroyed in the bombing and resultant fire which destroyed about 7/8 of the city. Thirty-six large bombers can make quite an impression on a small city like Singchang.

Dr. Yu made all the arrangements for us to get on the bus [for Chenghsien] the next morning and accompanied us to the station, seeing us safely on before he would return to his home."

Ken paid the men who had carried their belongings and the chair, grateful for their help. How relieved they were at the end of long days of walking, wrestling with their lone bicycle and riding in the sedan chair to be on a cramped bus. But to reach the home of Jack and Peggy Sharman where they believed they could rest for at least a few weeks and perhaps remain permanently was truly a blessing. The sight of Chenghsien, the city where he had first worked in China, however, saddened Ken. It was a changed city. On a later trip, he wrote, "Chenghsien was at that time about three-quarters ruined, and has since been almost completely wiped out by Japanese occupation."

The story of the carrier whom Ken tried to befriend, however, did not end there. Several months later when they were in another station, Linhai, with Mr. and Mrs. England, they heard about him again. Bessie England and Maybeth were walking down the street in the city when suddenly there was a great noise, shouting and yelling in the street coming their way. A crowd of people was swarming down the street. Maybeth asked Bessie what the crowd was about and she looked back and exclaimed, "Oh, dear, it's an execution again."

Public executions were very popular and always drew a crowd. The accused criminal was put in a chair and carried on the shoulders of the crowd to the outside of the city walls where he stood against the city wall and was shot. Usually his name and crime were written on a large placard and placed in front of him as he sat tied in the chair and paraded down the main street of the town. The townspeople considered it a holiday and joined in with glee and curiosity as the man was executed.

Bessie said, "Let's turn our backs to this and look in the store windows. We don't want to look at that fellow." So they did.

When the crowd seemed to be past, however, something prompted Maybeth to turn around and she realized that she could see the criminal very well. It was with horror and shock that she realized that she recognized him. She knew that she had seen him recently, but there had been so many strange faces that she had seen on their journey that she couldn't place who he might have been. He was somebody that she and Ken knew, somebody that they had talked to recently, somebody that they had become acquainted with. Maybeth marveled that someone she knew could be executed and she asked Bessie if she could read the sign that stated his crime, but it was too far away and she couldn't make it out. Soon the crowd went on by and out of the city and presently they heard the shot in the distance.

Maybeth went back to the house with Bessie that afternoon and told Ken about it. She knew they had known that man but could not place him. Later that afternoon Ken read the local Chinese paper and discovered that the man who had been executed had been a carrier. The story continued that this carrier had been carrying a Chinese man from the city where the Sharmans were, Chenghsien, to Ninghai. This passenger had apparently carried a small black bag, and the carrier, supposing that there was money in the bag, had killed him in the night as they slept and stolen his bag. Ironically, there was little in the bag, and after a brief flight into the hills, the carrier was captured by the police and brought to Linhai for execution. Suddenly Maybeth remembered him. He was the very man who had carried Gwen in the sedan chair a few months earlier. He was the surly one that Ken had tried to befriend.

How amazed they were that God had kept His hand of mercy on them while this same man had transported them across the same dangerous miles, sometimes with only Gwen in the chair and out of their sight altogether. How simple it would have been for him to kill them in the night as they all slept together on the pile of straw. How easily he could have kidnapped Gwen, their precious little girl. Most Chinese believed that the white man was wealthy and he could have taken their lives or taken Gwen hostage or worse. They knew that it was only the hand of God that had protected them from that evil on that perilous journey. In later years, Maybeth referred to this experience saying that sometimes when we pray for safety we never see those circumstances from which He is protecting us, but once in awhile, God seems to lift a corner of the veil that hides God's actions from man and show us how He is protecting us. Maybeth believed that often we have no idea how He protects us and cares for us. But this time He said, "See, that man could have killed you on the trip, and instead, in My mercy, you were kept safe."

Jack and Peggy Sharman welcomed the weary little family to Chenghsien with their own sweet charm. Concerned about them when they had heard of the last Japanese advance, they had contacted friends in Ninghai on the 9th of December and heard that the Grays had not arrived. Fearful that they were caught behind the Japanese lines, it was especially heartening to hear on the 10th that Ken and Maybeth had escaped the Japanese on bicycles.

Their arrival in Chenghsien on December 21st was a great event. The Welsh couple had a little boy, Hugh, who was almost the same age as Gwen. They had lost their first child, Katherine, the previous summer to dysentery. In the days before antibiotics and in remote cities of China, medicine for dysentery was nonexistent, and children particularly would simply waste away and die. Ken and Maybeth's hearts grieved for them in their loss, and it was good to spend some time with such good friends. Both Ken and Jack loved music and the chance to get together and sing some great old Welsh hymns was a treat for both. Ken played the piano and the rafters would ring with their voices. The Sharman's warmth and comfort to the weary travelers was indeed a gift of God.

The Sharman and Gray families at Christmas 1941. Left to right: Ken Gray, Maybeth Gray, Gwen Gray, Peggy Sharman, Hugh Sharman, Jack Sharman.

For Ken and Maybeth, it was a great relief to believe that they could stay awhile and work there in Chenghsien, safe from the advancing Japanese army. That the Japanese would be on their doorstep in a matter of months seemed impossible at the time. It was Christmas time and the families planned Christmas together. The company was so good and the two children loved having companions.

Ken wrote, "Across this picture of joy and happiness came an ugly shadow. One morning before breakfast a Jap plane came over the city and circled several times. It seemed to be an ill omen to us."

The next day, December 31, a day generally devoted to prayer in the China Inland Mission, they decided that it would be good to spend the day out in the hills that ringed the city, thanking God for the mercies of the previous year and praying that He would guide in the year to come. Spending time in the country also meant that the bombs wouldn't disrupt the day as they did in the city. The children could play and wouldn't need to be rushed to places of safety every time planes approached. The children had a wonderful time playing on the hills, and the two couples enjoyed the day also, away from the tension of the city. They went back into the city towards dark thinking that there was less likelihood of bombing in the evening.

CHAPTER SEVENTEEN

No sooner had they approached the city gates than they were greeted with rumors that the Japanese had made another westward push and were almost at the city gates. In fact, they were told that they were only 13 miles away. Their hearts sank realizing that they would have to leave in another mad rush. The Chinese characteristically fled before the advance of the Japanese army, fearing terrible reprisals and atrocities, as had happened in Nanking and other cities in the path of the Japanese advance. Almost all the people in the city were trying to escape the on-coming Japanese and take their precious possessions with them. Many had their valuables wrapped up in pieces of cloth and tied to a stick slung over their shoulders.

Quickly assessing the relative danger, Jack and Ken decided that all six of them must leave the city and so with heavy hearts they gathered together their possessions. Maybeth and Ken had barely unpacked theirs having arrived less than two weeks before, and their possessions were few, but the Sharmans had to go through the process of deciding what to take and what to leave. Finally, as darkness approached, they rushed down to the bus station. Twice that night, Peggy and Maybeth got on the bus with their children only to find that the men would not be allowed on. As the last bus filled up and Peggy and Maybeth again boarded it with their babies, a fat local banker rushed up to the bus. He convinced the driver that everyone should get off and that all luggage should be left and only the passengers get on the bus. This seemed like a good plan, and since they were the last on the bus, Maybeth and Peggy stepped down. No other passengers moved. The fat banker got on, took their places, and filled the extra seat with a box of hams that he had brought with him. The bus left almost immediately, leaving Maybeth and Peggy on the sidewalk.

It was close to midnight and as the last bus pulled out, they began to get desperate. The city was emptying, the rumors were flying that the Japanese would be entering the city at any moment and when they did Maybeth was sure they would be captured. Peggy and Maybeth stood at the empty bus station and prayed and Jack and Ken went all over the city looking for some means of transportation. Finally they decided that the women would begin the walk south down the road with a baby carriage with both babies in it and if Ken and Jack could not find any other help, they would catch up with them on the bicycles. Just as they were about to leave, a man who knew Jack slightly approached him. He was not a Christian, but Jack had been friendly with him. This man had a plan.

He owned a small charcoal-burning truck and he was leaving the city to go south toward Singchang. If they wanted to go, he said, the two women could ride in the cab of the truck with the driver, he would ride on the front fender holding a lantern, and Jack and Ken could ride their bikes alongside. Their few boxes, he said, could go in the back, already packed and crowded with his belongings. He warned that sometimes they would be driving without lights, and that his lantern would be the only light, but that it was a good move and his plan would take them a good distance away from the city. They were delighted and so thankful to God for His provision. Maybeth and Peggy climbed into the cab of the truck with the driver and held their toddlers on their laps. They were so grateful that the owner, who would have been riding where they were, had given up that place and was riding on the fender with a leg on each side of a headlight, a very precarious position. He held on to the headlight with one hand and to a rickety lamp with the other. Again they were reminded of the faithfulness of the God they served.

When they arrived in Singchang the next morning at 4:00 a.m., Dr. Yu, who had been so kind on their trip to Chenghsien two weeks earlier, met them. After about two hours of searching, their friend with the truck, who was going no further, finally found a man with a small open cart, more like a flat wheelbarrow, who agreed to take them further. Ken described that early January morning.

Just about then the Japanese guns started bombardment [of

Chenghsien] and we could hear the dull boom boom coming over the hills. The feeling it gave us was indescribable; just as though the whole bottom of things had dropped out again. However the carters soon came and action proved the only cure for the empty feeling which was not hunger.

At last we got everything safely onto the cart and started off at about 6:30 a.m. We had only gone a very short distance when we came to a narrow bridge and everything had to be unloaded again [to accommodate the bridge]. Just as we waited to get across the bridge, along came a long line of troops, and, of course, we had to wait until they got over first.

The cart was simply a flat board between two wheels with a man pulling it. Peggy and Maybeth sat back to back on the floorboard holding their children. There were no sides to the cart. The wheels would wobble and threaten to pitch them off into the mud. It was all they could do to stay on the bouncing cart and still hold their toddlers on their laps. Ken and Jack took turns riding Ken's bicycle alongside and walking, Jack's bicycle having broken down. Their baggage was piled high on the cart and sometimes Jack would lie on the top of the luggage on the cart. When the road went up the mountains, everyone would get off the cart and help push on up the hill. Ken would take little Gwen on his bicycle and they would wait for the others at the top of the hill. Ken so appreciated Gwen's sweet trusting attitude in this hectic pace. She would stand at the top of the hill and toss small stones down the side to watch them bounce off the rocks. Then she would see her mama and call out to her. She was a perfect example of a child who had complete trust in her parents and Ken, seeing her, prayed that he would have that kind of trust in the God who had saved them to this point.

They traveled like that for two days. Cold weather had set in; terribly cold; so very very cold. They slept in dirty inns at night. There were pigs on the floor beneath them. The upper floor was simply slats and everything fell through down to the pigpen. It was a difficult journey, filled with fear that the Japanese would catch them at any time. Many refugees were traveling the same road and the inns were crowded. It was a blessing simply to find a place to lie down at night. How happy Ken and Maybeth were for the company of Jack and Peggy Sharman on such a difficult trip. Jack's sense of humor and calm disposition made troubles disappear and the trip look like an adventure.

Their progress was periodically halted when planes would circle slowly over them. It was customary for the Japanese to machine gun the roads if there were people on them and so everyone on the road made for the ditch and lay there praying that they would not be machine gunned. The road wound through valleys and along hillsides and there were often gravestones along the roadside. As the planes approached, the refugees on the road would hide behind the more imposing gravestones, reasonable shelter from strafing airplanes. The two couples and their children soon learned the procedure and dashed for the biggest gravestone they could find, but frequent strafing by the Japanese made an already difficult trip longer and more stressful.

As the party of six traveled they met many fellow refugees traveling the same roads. One of these refugees was a beautiful Chinese girl. She was a Christian and they quickly grew to love her. She was probably in her late teens but she was so different from the other refugees they had met on their flight from the Japanese. Most of the others were not interested in anything but their own safety and security and had no time to talk about God. This young woman was confident in the providence of God and spoke freely to the missionary families of that hope. She was a blessing to their hungry souls.

The weather continued cold, and rain fell sporadically. Gwen caught a cold. She ate a little food and then brought it up and it dirtied the front of her quilted jacket. Maybeth didn't dare take it off because of the cold and she had no other warm garment to put on her. Her mother's heart hurt for Gwen as, cuddled close in her arms, she struggled to breathe freely.

They traveled south on the cart and bicycle, following the winding road and staying in wayside inns overnight, and arrived in the small town of Tientai late one evening. They knew that there was a house belonging to the Mission there and hoped that they could have a place to rest. All the way the weather was cold and wet, and all six were shivering and exhausted. Maybeth did her best to keep Gwen warm, but the soaking rain thoroughly chilled them all. The Japanese had pushed closer to Chengshien after they left, but the Chinese army had pushed them back so there was a good distance between the Japanese and the fleeing refugees. The four exhausted missionaries and their two children were glad for a chance to stop and rest. They were taken in by the single lady missionary, an American lady, who lived and worked in Tientai.

Gwen had a little cough that didn't bother her except at night and she so enjoyed the release from being held in her mother's lap for hours of the day. She ran around in the sun in a new little quilted coat that Ken bought for her and thrilled her parents with her sweet, happy nature. There was a cat in the yard and she loved playing with it on the porch in the noontime sunshine. There was time to read to her and show her pictures and even a little rocking chair that she would rock vigorously back and forth. The cough was worrisome though, and Maybeth gave her some cough mixture and asked that a stove be put into the room where she slept so that she would be warm at night.

But a day or two after their arrival, Gwen's cough became worse and she had some difficulty breathing that evening. By midnight Ken and Maybeth became frightened and called in a Chinese doctor, Dr. Ting, who was trained in Shanghai. He said she had pneumonia, but that they shouldn't worry, for she would get well again. He gave her injections of medicine and it seemed to help her breathing for a while. All that night Ken and Maybeth sat up with her by the stove, putting on a mild mustard plaster and giving her medicine.

She was worse again the next day, January 5, and they sent again for the doctor. He came and gave her further injections. That morning Maybeth sat beside her mattress on the floor holding her precious child's hands and Gwen would pull her down and put her cheek against Maybeth's. She couldn't eat and she was finding it increasingly hard to breathe. Ken telegrammed through to the next city, Linhai, where a missionary couple, the Englands, were, and told them of their trouble. Bessie England replied that she would come up by boat as soon as possible within the next two days and help Maybeth nurse Gwen so that she could take turns and get some rest.

But that late morning, Gwen began to have spells of unconsciousness. When the doctor came again at noon, she lost consciousness and before one o'clock that afternoon she had passed away to be with the God who made her and loved her. Ken and Maybeth knelt beside her, holding her hands and praying, and she quietly slipped away from them into eternity. Ken closed her eyes and she was gone.

Maybeth wrote to her father and mother about it all saying,

We could only pray that the Lord's will be done, and if he could spare her yet to us, we would be so happy. But he wanted her, and through our tears and with breaking hearts, we could say from our hearts, "The Lord giveth and the Lord taketh away; blessed be the name of the Lord." Oh it was so hard, but He did give grace and strength.... It was all so sudden – she was only really sick just over half a day and we just couldn't realize that she had really left us for glory. But we liked to think of her being welcomed in heaven by the Lord and by Ken's little mother who went up there so short a time ago and by Katherine Sharman, who was just Gwen's age.

Ken and Maybeth were overwhelmed. Ken wrote, "The light went out of her eyes and, it seemed, out of our life." There was nothing they could have done. The nearest missionary doctor was six days traveling away and it all had happened so fast. They stood there and looked down at little Gwen who was not quite two years old. Her birthday was January 25. Someone had given her a little white toy rabbit and Maybeth had given it to her early before her birthday because she thought it would make the trip easier. After she died, Maybeth dressed her in a pink silk dress appliquéd with many flowers that had been given to them in Shaoxing. It was a dress that Gwen had always loved and she would laugh and be so delighted whenever she wore it. They put the little toy rabbit in her arms.

Ken and Jack Sharman found some wood at that Mission station to make a casket. They made it out of rough-hewn boards. As Maybeth stood watching Ken make a casket, she asked the inevitable, "Why?"

"Why does God allow this to happen to us? God, we're serving You; why do You allow this to happen to us? Couldn't You protect her or heal her?"

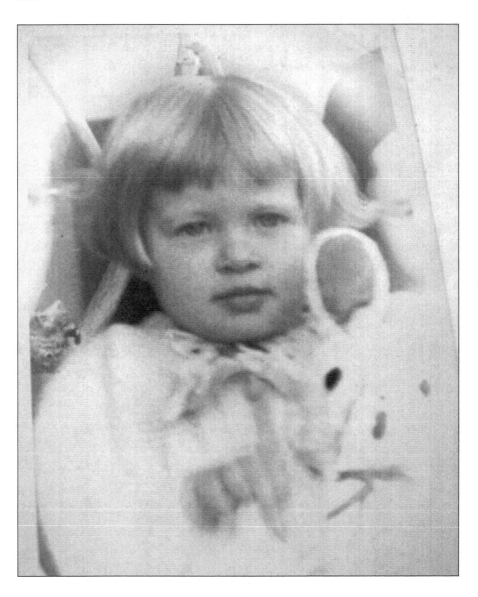

Gwen and her favorite toy in 1941.

115

Ken comforted her as well as he could through his own grief,

The only thing I know is that God is Love and we have to trust Him. When John, the Baptist, said, "Why am I still in prison when You are healing the sick and making the blind see?" The answer was, "Trust me." We are asked to trust in the most desperate places of our lives. He didn't say "Trust me," in so many words to John the Baptist, but He said, "I know your situation." The Lord was quite aware of John the Baptist's peril. There is one thing that we can do; one thing will honor God; and that is to trust Him. We don't know why he allowed this.

The Sharmans were a wonderful gift. Although they had gone back to their mission station in Chengshien a day earlier, they immediately returned at the news to be with Ken and Maybeth and to share their grief. Jack Sharman didn't need to say a word. He came into the room, put his hand on Ken's shoulder and said, "I know what you feel." Somehow that hand on his shoulder of someone who had recently gone through such an experience meant more than all the sympathy letters and cards that others could give. Jack and Peg could identify with them and it meant the world to both Ken and Maybeth right then.

The townspeople there in Tientai, when Ken asked if they could bury their daughter, said, "No, we don't want any foreign devils in our cemetery." ("foreign devils" at that time was simply an expression, but often folks would call it out after foreigners when they went out in the street or anywhere in the city.) Tientai was a strongly Buddhist city and they had no foreign cemetery.

As they grieved and wondered what to do next, there was a knock at the door. It was the young Christian refugee woman whom they had come to love on the trip. She put a brown paper parcel into Maybeth's hands and said, "I want you to have this."

Maybeth opened the parcel and took out a long length of beautiful brocade blue silk. She said, "What is this?"

"It is my wedding dress material," she said. "I've saved it in every flight from the Japanese. It is the most precious thing I have, but I want you to have it to line the baby's casket. You love God and I love God. We're in one family. Please let me do this for you, for Jesus sake."

Maybeth took the silk and she and Ken thanked her from overflowing hearts. They could hardly speak for the tears in their eyes and the lumps in their throats. Ken took that gorgeous silk and lined the casket with it, fastening it along the sides and top.

The next day they had to tell the Englands so that Bessie wouldn't make the trip upriver. Frank and Bessie England insisted that Ken and Maybeth come on downriver to them in Linhai where they could rest and where Gwen could be buried in the Christian cemetery.

That night around 9:30, Ken and Maybeth took Gwen in the casket in a tiny rowboat, along with the bicycle and went downriver to where there was a Christian church and a Christian cemetery. The Chinese boatmen were very superstitious and would not think of taking a corpse, so they wrapped Gwen's tiny coffin in a rug, one that people typically wrapped around their belongings and, accompanied by their dear friends, Jack and Peggy Sharman, headed for Linhai. They floated lazily down the river all that day and what a sad day it was; how heartbroken they were as they sat silently hardly able to speak with the little casket between them and the bicycle behind them.

They arrived in Linhai the next day in the early evening and Frank and Bessie England and a Chinese group from the church there met them at the riverside. Mr. Eddie Smythe, a fellow missionary of the CIM, had walked almost 30 miles to be there for the funeral. It was still raining and cold, but the people that met them were brothers and sisters. Although the Chinese Christians had never seen Ken and Maybeth before, they lavished love on them. They had dug the grave and they had brought some artificial flowers.

The missionaries, Mr. and Mrs. England, were another gift of God. They buried Gwen there in that lonely wet hillside which was the Christian cemetery. It was hardly even a proper cemetery, just a hillside in the pouring rain, late at night, with folks carrying lanterns. Bessie England made a wreath for Maybeth to put on the grave of small pink roses and fragrant Chinese lilies. Bessie also laid a wreath of lilies.

The service was conducted in both Chinese and English. Some of the Chinese Christians sang and they read the Scripture together as they stood around the casket. Ken had always felt that it was a good thing to sing at a funeral, but the lump in his throat prevented him from singing and almost from speaking. It was a memorable scene on that cold, wet January evening as they stood on that lonely hillside, touched by the love of strangers. Gwen was buried beside the graves of early missionaries, Mr. and Mrs. Rudland and their little daughter. All around were graves of Chinese Christians and in the distance the hills loomed. It was hard to bury their little Gwen there knowing they would never see her again on this earth. They also knew that it wasn't really her; it was merely a shell. They knew that she was with the Lord. They had a small stone made for her with the following engraving: "Till He Come, Gwen Enid Gray, Born Jan 25, 1940, Died Jan 5, 1942." Underneath in Chinese was a verse from Scripture "To depart and be with Christ which is far better."

Not far away on the same hillside was a "baby tower" where unwanted live Chinese baby girls were thrown. Maybeth understood that it was still in use. She couldn't help but compare those poor little unwanted girls cast in there to die, with her Gwen, whom she loved so fiercely and missed so much. How awful it must be, she thought, to be so unwanted and unloved. Though her heart ached for Gwen it was good to know with certainty that someday she would see her, never to part again. Ken and Maybeth never went back to Linhai again; they had no opportunity.

PART FOUR - STAYING A STEP AHEAD OF THE ENEMY

"When through fiery trials your pathway shall lie,
My grace, all sufficient, shall be your supply.
The flame shall not hurt you; I only design
Your dross to consume and your gold to refine."

CHAPTER EIGHTEEN

Frank and Bessie England, the missionaries they stayed with in Linhai after the death of Gwen, became true friends,. She was Scottish and he was English. They had belonged to the Plymouth Brethren church before they came to China, but had moved away from the Brethren and attended Anglican services, preferring the worshipful attitude of the Anglican service over the more unstructured worship of the Brethren. They were in their late thirties, and had never had any children of their own, although they had always wished for them. They were devastated over Ken and Maybeth's loss of Gwen. On the trip from Chenghsien downriver to Linhai, Ken and Maybeth had lost or left behind everything they had picked up on their flight from Fenghua, leaving them with practically no belongings, but the Englands shared. Bessie opened her closet and said, "Come on, Maybeth. You take a dress or two and some sweaters." Ken took a suit from Frank's closet though Frank was much larger than Ken. The tired and heartsick Grays were loved and comforted by these dear friends. It was fairly quiet in Linhai with little bombing and no immediate threat of a Japanese invasion. Ken and Maybeth forever appreciated the Englands' love and understanding and the relative quiet of that city. Ken wrote,

...so began, right in one of the darkest hours of our lives, ...a time which we shall remember as one of the happiest. As we lived with Frank and Bessie England and made arrangements about a small stone for Gwen's grave, we found out that we could live without her, and that we still found that God was love. The sun shone again. Flowers still bloomed; we could even laugh. At first we could not speak of Gwen, for our throats choked up. Later we found, with the help of Frank and Bessie that we could talk about her, and that bye and bye we wanted to

talk about her. So she lives in that ever green field of memory where she is always young, and so very loveable.

Linhai was an ancient city with a milder climate than they were used to and they enjoyed the history of the city set in the hills of central Zhejiang province. It boasted an ancient wall, called the southern Great Wall, for protection from barbarians. The church was quite active having been visited early in the history of the CIM by a missionary family, the Rudlands.

Frank and Bessie gave both Ken and Maybeth work to do. Recently Linhai had suffered a tremendous flood and the river had flooded their living room three-quarters of the way up the walls. The couch was destroyed and so was much of the other furniture with the soaking of the filthy water. But they hoped to save a small pump organ that they had used for their own use and for services in the church nearby. They asked Ken if he could try to fix it, and he went to work on it immediately, taking it all apart and buying new felt for the stops. He took it out on the porch into the sunshine, drying out each piece and gluing the new felt. It took him about a month to complete and involved his concentration. At the end he had a beautifully restored organ which the Englands were delighted to be able to use again.

Meanwhile Maybeth was set to the task of pulling bookworms out of a lot of old and valuable books that had been left on that mission station. She sat on the porch and hooked the bookworms with a little wire hook and destroyed them. Although the bookworms had turned some of the pages into powder, if she got the worms out before they had a chance to nest and multiply, there was a chance the books would be saved. So day by day Maybeth would sit in the February sunshine on the porch and hook worms and Ken would work on the organ. Sharing meals with the Englands and with time and work to do, they began to heal.

Frank England was a big-hearted person. His Chinese was terrible; he never could master the language, but the people loved him. Once he told Ken, "I want these new Christians to be more reverent in church. The children are running up and down the aisles in church, peeling their oranges or running in and out of the door. It's hard to get a sense of reverence. Their behavior is not out of disregard, but simply because they don't know better." Frank had tried to instill his Anglican sense of worship into the service, but the Chinese continued to talk and shell peanuts and allow their children to run around. So he discussed a plan with Ken. His plan was to begin each worship service with the words, "HOLY, HOLY, HOLY" to try to give the congregation a sense of true reverence.

The next Sunday Ken and Maybeth sat in church with the Chinese congregation and Frank came solemnly to the front of the room and stood quietly a minute. Then, instead of announcing a hymn as he usually did, he raised his hands and said Chinese words that sounded like "Holy" a little bit but without an aspirant and a change in tone. What he actually was saying was something like "Fresh vegetables, Fresh vegetables, Fresh vegetables." And then he began to preach the sermon. The congregation was so polite and they loved Frank so much, they never even cracked a smile. Ken got to know some of the people and talked with one of the young men in the church whose comment was, "Frank really loves us; he can't speak our language well, but he loves us and we love him." Frank was very much loved all over that part of China. He was truly a Godly man. Two months later, in April, after Ken and Maybeth left them, he and Bessie were to become instrumental in saving American airmen from the Japanese as described in the book *Thirty Seconds over Tokyo* by Ted W. Lawson. Chinese fishermen brought downed airmen to their home and, risking imprisonment and even death, they found them medical help and eventually arranged for transportation out of the area to safety.

About three months later, near the end of March of 1942, the CIM leaders decided that Ken and Maybeth needed to get out of that area of the country, further away from danger. Maybeth discovered that she was pregnant and it was better to be west where there was more chance of peace and quiet. Maybeth was so very grateful to know that God was going to give them another child. Not wanting to take any unnecessary risks and yet still planning to work for God, they decided that they would go west to avoid the Japanese invasion of the coastal region.

They hoped that they could get far enough away so that if they needed to settle down sometime later in the pregnancy, they would have some assurance of safety.

Sending a carrier with their belongings to head for the city of Yongkang, they followed on two bikes, each with a basket. The carriers were very honest. Ken could give them two big trunks and tell them where he would meet them at the end of the day and when he and Maybeth arrived, they would be there waiting. They spent their first night with friends, the Smythes, and as they departed the next day Frances Smythe packed them two days food.

They put what they could into the two baskets on the bicycles, leaving the carriers to bring the rest. They came to the high mountains dividing East and West Zhejiang on the second day out. Worn in body, newly pregnant and heartsick still over the loss of her little girl, Maybeth became periodically overpoweringly tired and disheartened. Once or twice she stopped by the side of the road and told Ken, "I can't go a step further. I really can't. I'm just too tired."

Ken understood that they had to keep going, so he would get quite firm with her. Although he also was weary and still suffering the loss of Gwen, he'd say, "Come on. You've got to keep going. Get up!"

So Maybeth would get up and hope for a downhill stretch, although there seemed to be very few of those. Ken wrote,

Up and up again we went, and we were surely glad when we reached the top of the hill at about mid-day. We went on from the small village at the top and with a wonderful panoramic view of much of the west below us, we ate the good lunch which Frances had put up for our second day out... As we sat there looking out over our new field of labour, we wondered what was in store for us. We may have thought of many things. But what was in store was mercifully hid from our eyes.

The country around Yongkang was much different than they were used to: much flatter than in the east of the province, with great rolling plains, sparsely scattered with dwarf pine and a scattering of underbrush. When they reached Yongkang, they were directed to the house owned by the CIM. It was empty as the missionary couple that would normally have been there had left for Ningbo hurriedly when the woman had suffered appendicitis. While at the Baptist hospital in Ningbo, the city fell into Japanese hands and there was no way they could return. In fact, they were confined to a prison camp as many other missionaries were at this time. They had a little girl, their first child, and Ken and Maybeth arrived about two months after they had left. The house was left just as they had used it since they had planned to be gone for only a short time.

No one had taken care of the house and Ken and Maybeth found it in a bit of a mess. The jam in the closets had popped the lids and the butter was rancid in the pantry. Even the clothes had moths in them. Every time Maybeth opened a closet, the moths swarmed out and she found wool clothing eaten through with moth holes. There were quite a few usable things however, and knowing that these missionaries would not be returning in the foreseeable future, Ken and Maybeth helped themselves. There were some treasures left in their cupboards; there was brown sugar, white sugar and other treasures. Maybeth also picked up several baby garments left behind, the child having outgrown them, and some household items. During this time of refugee flight, all the missionaries of the various missionary societies had developed this sharing relationship and Maybeth was glad to be able to pick up some clothes for the next baby along the way. Here was another provision of God since she had no baby things at all, Gwen's having been lost in the flight from Fenghua.

While Ken and Maybeth were in Yongkang, the war raged in the Pacific. Japanese troops surged through Southeast Asia. The Bataan Death March shocked the world and within days of the surrender of troops in Bataan, Doolittle's raiders launched the first retaliatory air attack on Japan since the Pearl Harbor attack. Sixteen army B-25 bombers were launched from an aircraft carrier and flew missions over Tokyo bombing major cities. After the bombs were dropped, the planes were scheduled to land in Free China. Many ran low on fuel and crash landed in the sea or on the coast in Japanese-occupied territory. The book, *Thirty Seconds over Tokyo* is the story of one of those bomber pilots who was sheltered by the Englands in Linhai. The Japanese in China were enraged at the audacity of the Chinese to shelter these pilots and increased their bombing of cities, particularly cities that were said to have protected the American pilots.

At the same time the Japanese army fought on, taking Corregidor and seeming to be invincible. Ken and Maybeth hoped that America would turn its attention to China soon because it seemed that the Chinese could not possibly hold out against the superior Japanese forces. China's great asset was its patience and tolerance of hardship. War was a fact of life. The peasants did not know any other life and expected to be uprooted with each new wave of fighting. The Chinese did not expect a victory would come easily, so they settled in for the long haul hoping for help from somewhere. Sooner or later, they believed, the Allies would overcome, although at this moment the future looked bleak.

The situation in the city was precarious with frequent bombings, although the Japanese army was some distance away. The church in that city was in need of some encouragement, and so Ken and Maybeth decided to stay there and work as long as they could. The two-story house had its own quaint charm. It had electricity, the first they had enjoyed on a mission station, but it was limited to only one bulb per household. The bulb was on a long extension cord and whenever they moved from room to room they took the light with them. They felt that it was a true luxury to have electric light, so never minded moving it around from room to room. Of course the cord only reached into the downstairs rooms. Upstairs they were in darkness.

This house also had an inside toilet, a rarity. It wasn't much; just a bucket they had to dump every day, but it seemed luxurious not to have to go outside as they were used to. The toilet had another amenity. The tiny room had been wallpapered with front covers of the Saturday Evening Post. Most of the pictures were Norman Rockwell paintings which Maybeth grew to love. The prints were so typical of life in the United States and painted with such a whimsical approach to normal life. In a time when life was anything but normal for Maybeth, Norman Rockwell made it seem like being home and safe. She could look at those paintings and believe that there was another world, far removed from the frightening reality of bombs and the life of a refugee. Someday she hoped to see that world again, but the chances of getting through this war without being eventually captured by the Japanese seemed very slim at times. She was tired of moving, tired of running, and sometimes just wanted to escape from the present into a time when life was more homespun as Rockwell's paintings depicted.

The house had a substantial dugout in the back yard which they used for a bomb shelter. Feeling quite fortunate, they settled in there, believing that they might be able to attain a measure of permanence. There was a small garden in the back yard and the church was next door.

Yongkang was well known for the strangeness of the dialect and they found it very difficult to communicate with the people there at first. Ken and to some extent, Maybeth, did begin to learn it, and it was a blessing to them to be able to minister to the people in that city. Both Ken and Maybeth felt that they had had little opportunity to teach the Chinese people about the God whom they loved and to lead them to an understanding of God. For many months now they felt they had not ministered to anyone as they fled for their lives. They longed to teach and preach as they had in Fenghua those first few years. But the political situation had prevented their work and now it felt good to settle down again and do what they had come to China to do. It had been more than four months since that fateful day when the BBC had announced the attack at Pearl Harbor and Ken and Maybeth hadn't been able to settle down anywhere since then.

They weren't bombed very much, but now and again the alarm would sound and they would go down into the dugout and wait for the all clear sound. A nearby city held a Baptist hospital where there were several missionaries with whom they developed a good friendship. (One was named John Davis and they always referred to him as John the Baptist.) Ken planted a garden and they looked forward to the fresh vegetables they would soon have. Maybeth worked to clean up the house and rid it of pests, and soon it felt like home. What a blessing it seemed to be able to settle down and live a more normal life! Ken, an inveterate farmer wrote,

We got things planted in the garden. The plums, oranges and peaches gave good promise of a good crop; we had lots of small cucumbers for pickles, tomatoes, corn and good squash; everything seemed to be just as we wanted it. There was plenty of work for us to do. Some 2000 Chinese met in the 25 meeting places in the district, and one could safely say that most of these knew little of the fundamental doctrines of the Christian faith.

One evening in late April, the local magistrate paid a call with exciting news. He invited Ken and Maybeth to a feast at his house to honor a group of the pilots from Doolittle's Raiders. Ken and Maybeth went with delight to meet the young men who had landed near Yongkang. They thoroughly enjoyed the young men and enjoyed catching up on news of the war and of home. These pilots were so clean cut and polite and gave Ken and Maybeth a refreshing lift from their daily routine. Ken, particularly, enjoyed talking with them about their planes and their training. It was good to talk English and to be able to communicate with someone without the struggle of speaking a foreign language.

Since they appeared to be settled, the Mission directors asked Ken if he would take on the area local secretary position, and invited him and Maybeth to Kinhwa to learn the duties.

Shortly before we were forced to leave Yongkang, we were asked to go to Kinhwa for a visit. One morning good and early Maybeth and I started off on our cycles, and through the clear morning air made good time over the good motor road which went to Kinhwa. It was a real treat for us to cycle on a motor road for hitherto we had nothing better than cobblestone paths, which the Chinese call roads.

Kinhwa presented a formidable appearance with machine gun emplacements all over the place, and soldiers working on the old walls of the city making more. Kinhwa was in those days a little Shanghai. You could buy everything on the street, but it took lots of money. There were lovely oiled silk raincoats, rubberized ones, shoes galore, good stationery, fountain pens, and what not, but all at a terrible price. We did not do much purchasing, but did get a few things which would be handy later on. Little did we think that in a short time the city would be empty, and then in a few more days occupied by the Japanese.

After getting briefly initiated in the Local Secretary work, we took to the road to return to Yongkang. When we were not very far from Yongkang, we suddenly heard what we thought were some heavy trucks coming up behind us, and upon looking back found it was six Jap bombers. We no sooner had dived to the side of the road than we heard a heavy rumble of bombs. We found out afterward they fell just about half a mile behind us on the motor road.

We arrived back in Yongkang to find the city all in a stir. The four big banks were packing up to flee the city for safer cities further west. We thought, however, that it was only a local thing like many others before it, and that when the Japanese met with some resistance, they would not come further. We were under the impression that there were some very good troops guarding the line. Both our suppositions were wrong, however, for the troops had been withdrawn to meet a thrust toward Changsha, and the soldiers which were left did not offer any resistance to the Japanese till they reached Kinhwa. Then it was too late.

CHAPTER NINETEEN

Ken, in the short time he had been in the city, had come to know the magistrate, or city manager, quite well and so he asked him where he and Maybeth could find a cart and a coolie to pull it if they should have to leave. The magistrate assured them that he would have one for them and that they were not to worry.

The next day the rumors expanded and grew and still they waited for their friend, the magistrate, to send the cart. Friends and neighbors came by to ask when they were leaving, and still they waited for word from the magistrate. Afternoon came and finally Ken walked to his house and politely asked him when the cart might be available. The magistrate said, offhandedly, that the cart would be there first thing the next morning. It was hard to tell how close the Japanese were. Ken knew that if they were as close as the rumors claimed, he and Maybeth would have to flee before the next morning, and he didn't know how they would get very far with one bicycle between them [their other one broken beyond repair]. But there was nothing else to do except wait. Most of the population in the city was leaving and all available transportation was taken. Ken went out in the street and purchased another bike, a ramshackle old man's bike without fenders, and they determined that if they had to, they would leave their belongings and hope the cart would follow them south toward Lishui where they would go on the bicycles.

It was an anxious day. The rumors swirled around them, but they knew that there was nothing more they could do except wait and listen to any official news. That afternoon and evening Ken suggested that they use up some of the sugar and other goods that were in the house. It seemed a shame to leave it there, and activity helped with their fears, so together they made two huge batches of fudge with some cocoa left in the house. They put the fudge in round cake pans. Ken stood over an old stove and stirred the fudge, rushing out periodically to the dugout where he could hear official bulletins or news on the radio about the proximity of the Japanese. That night was taken up with final packing and periodically checking for official warnings.

The next morning, true to his word, the magistrate sent a coolie to the door with a cart to carry their belongings. Ken wrote of that morning,

Just as we were loading up the cart, the cry came, "Planes" and we hurriedly ran to the shelter in the corner of the garden. It was a lovely corner, for the former missionary had planted blue iris all over the top of the dug-out, and it was in a corner of the garden shaded almost entirely by peach and plum trees, so it was like a little arbour. The planes came, three of them, and as a last gesture before leaving dropped a large bundle of anti-British/American pamphlets in our garden. We thought we were surely going to get the "goods" when that plane came swooping down on us and we could hear the swish of a falling object. Fortunately for us it was "bomphlets" rather than the real thing.

Maybeth couldn't decide the best way to carry the fudge. Whenever they had to travel by bike they tried to carry as much as they could, so Maybeth had made tote bags that attached to the crossbar on the bike. These bags hung from the bar and extended to the gear wheel at the bottom of the frame of the bike. They packed the cart with their accumulated belongings and, as a last minute decision, decided to each put a pan of the fudge in the bottom of the bag along with other items they might need on the ride. Heavily laden and anxious, they started out on the trek. Periodically they would stop and wait for the coolie pulling the cart, since it was much more slow going for him.

It was a terribly hot day in early June. The road followed a river and the sun beat down on them as they cycled along the river valley. Frequently planes flew over causing the people crowding the roads to head quickly for the ditch. Most of the bombers who targeted the roads also sent a blast of machine-gun fire to punish the refugees who were fleeing. Maybeth, five months pregnant, felt the vicious heat and frequently had to stop and rest. After the day had reached it's hottest,

Maybeth began to wonder why her legs were so wet and sticky. Of course, the fudge, firm and cool in the morning, had melted as the day wore on and run down, oozing through the cloth bag and on to her legs every time she made a revolution with the pedal. There was nothing to do but throw it away and take a few licks of a sticky pan. Throwing away the precious fudge, they laughed at themselves and the mess they had created. Both had legs and hands and even faces, sticky with the chocolate fudge and no place to clean up.

Sticky and hot, they arrived at Tsinyuin (Jinyan), twenty miles down the river road. There they were welcomed into the home of the Maags, a charming and gracious Swiss missionary couple. Ken knew Mr. Maag quite well although it was the first time Maybeth had met either of them. As Swiss nationals they were considered neutral parties. They were staying where they were and didn't need to fear Japanese occupation. Also staying in the station was a German couple, the Hohermuths who were also good friends of Ken's. They also had nothing to fear from the Japanese since Germany and Japan were allies in the war. They had come to Tsinyuin for supplies and had left their children in their own mission station some distance away in care of a single lady missionary and so were anxious to get back so that they would not be separated from their children. Ken wrote of the home of the Swiss missionaries, the Maags,

We were dirty, tired, and hungry, and we stepped out of the warm day into coolness and an immaculately clean household. We were then shown to our room, where the windows were framed in white starched curtains, where the floor was as clean as a new pin, and that evening after a restful afternoon, and good meals we lay down on a comfortable bed between spotlessly clean linen sheets.

Maybeth and Ken were overwhelmed by the gracious hospitality shown by these Swiss missionaries in taking them in, cleaning them up and giving them such a reception and a good meal. It seemed that the Japanese, focused on taking Yongkang, were staying well behind them , and so they felt a real sense of relief and comfort in that lovely home for the night. Weary and a bit dispirited, they lost no time in drifting off to a much-needed sleep.

133

Tsinyuin however, would not be a refuge for long. Ken wrote,

The following day we thought we could stay there, and wait to see if the Japanese thrust was going to develop into a large action, or if it was of a local nature. During the day a plane came over a few times; once two came and tried to bomb the large bridge over the river leading out of the city. They missed the bridge, but one plane circled the city, let off a few bursts of machine-gun fire just over the house and gave us a scare, sending us scuttling for shelter behind the thickest walls! That evening we went down to the telephone office to find out as much as we could about the situation. The head man there said little but thought the Japs were about 10 miles away from the city. As we left, he was very polite (so we thought) and followed us out into the dark outer court of the house and said, " I didn't like to say much inside, but Yongkang fell to the Japs just a little while ago."

We planned to get up early and get on the road by at least 5 a.m. so that we could get the most of the journey over before the heat of the day and before the planes got too active.

They hadn't been in bed more than an hour, however, when an alarm went off in the city, and Mr. Maag came to warn them that they would have to leave because the Japanese had unexpectedly pushed on after taking Yongkang and would arrive in Tsinyuin any time.

It was midnight, but Mr. Maag told them that Herman Hohermuth and his wife were also leaving and suggested that they go together. "You'll be company for one another," he said, "and if you should run into any Japanese anywhere along the road, you just stay close to the German couple and they will be some protection for you." Mr. Maag, the Swiss friend, came along with them at least for the beginning of the trip because he thought he could help keep them safe using his neutral status.

CHAPTER TWENTY

Once more they dragged their weary bodies to the bicycles and headed south to Lishui, nearly twenty miles away. Two miles south along the road at midnight, they encountered the Chinese army. In an attempt to prevent or at least slow down the advance of the Japanese army, the Chinese were breaking up the road so that the Japanese wouldn't be able to bring their guns and equipment along it. The government of the town had called out all able-bodied Chinese to dig trenches to prevent Japanese invasion. Apparently the entire town was there in the middle of the night. They dug trenches several feet deep and about every hundred yards across the road. The little party edged forward, their cart piled high with their belongings and some belongings of the Hohermuth's also, and four bicycles trying to negotiate the road! Mr. Maag, a spry old man of at least 75 or 80 years old, somehow found two long planks and carried them along as he accompanied them in the pitch darkness. He would lay the planks across the trench, and the Grays and the Hohermuths would push the four bicycles across the trench. Then the man pulling the cart would go across, and Mr. Maag would pick up the planks. Then he would drag the planks along and they would walk about a hundred yards and he would put the planks down again and they would wheel the bicycles across. They continued in this labored way for almost four hours during the night.

The scene along the road was unreal and nightmarish. The Chinese, as they dug the trenches, made great bonfires so that they could see to work. Between the bonfires, the night was pitch black with overcast skies and no light at all. They were six people with bicycles and a cart amid hundreds of others either fleeing along with them or working to destroy the road. As they stumbled along the narrow, treacherous road winding along a steep hillside, they were literally bumping elbows with others flooding the road with them. Periodically the bonfires lit up the night. The Chinese took bundles of straw and tied them tightly together and made makeshift torches to light their work. Hundreds of Chinese civilians had been forced to cut the trenches across the road, lit only by the yellow-orange flame of burning straw torches. The road snaked along the side of the hills with hairpin turns as it wound up and down the steep hillsides. One side dropped into a deep canyon down to the river at the bottom, so they had to make sure they were well clear of the edge. The damp night air, the glowing torches and orange glow of the bonfires and the hundreds of refugees walking silently along, was a sight indelibly etched in Maybeth's mind.

Negotiating the ditches made for slow going and their progress seemed almost nonexistent as they walked and pushed bicycles. Finally they reached the end of the damaged road, Mr. Maag turned back to go home, and the four cyclists forged ahead on a stretch of road that was free of trenches. They could cycle along more quickly once free of the ditches, but it was still pitch dark, and they had to be careful of the edge of the trail. One cyclist would go in front with the tiny lantern and the others would follow watching the lantern and not the road. Often they would stop just in time to save running into some weary walkers or a cart being pulled along in the pitch darkness. Still the road was packed with many Chinese refugees traveling on foot, on bicycles, or in rickshaws. Ken wrote,

It was most strenuous, and our nerves were like a taut wire. No one else had a light, but the road was almost filled with refugees. Occasionally a car or a truck would come from Lishui to try to get some more goods away from the city, and shortly would come back again. We crouched against the banks of the road to escape being run down by these motors driven at top speed along the narrow road.

Once the road cleared up, Ken told the man pulling the cart to keep pulling as best he could through the night and that they would go ahead and meet him in the morning light. He had proven extremely reliable, and Ken paid him well. Twice that night a Nationalist Army roadblock

136

stopped them. Ken and Maybeth went in front and showed their Canadian passports and in that way the Hohermuths would come along also and not be taken captive by the Nationalist troops.

Eventually the Hohermuths, faster cyclists than Ken and especially Maybeth, went ahead to find lodging for them all in Lishui, and Ken and Maybeth came along later. Maybeth was very tired; she didn't feel very well because of her pregnancy and her pace was slower. As the sun slowly lighted up the sky, both Ken and Maybeth felt enormously grateful to God for his faithful protection and loving care of them. What a joy it was to see the sun and realize that the night that had been so harrowing and had seemed to last so long, was over.

As morning broke, Ken felt they should stop and wait for the cart. They stopped by a small, three-room Chinese hut with a bench outside. The lady of the house was up already and sweeping the road in front of her house in the morning light. As she swept, she saw the two weary travelers come along the road. They hadn't slept at all that night and the night had had its share of fears and dangers. Ken, concerned about Maybeth's weariness and discomfort, approached the woman and said, "Do you mind if my wife sits on your bench and has a rest?"

The lady looked at Maybeth and at once saw that she was pregnant, exhausted, and a refugee. She said, "Don't sit on my bench; come into my home and sleep on my bed."

Her generosity overwhelmed Maybeth, bringing quick tears to her eyes, as this stranger took her into her house, brought her a cup of hot tea, laid her down on her big Chinese brick bed, and put her own quilt over her, murmuring comforting words as she did. Ken sat outside on the bench to catch the coolie, but Maybeth, who could always sleep anywhere, enjoyed an hour or so of good sleep there because of the kindness of a woman who had no idea who they were and would never know. Maybeth was so grateful to think that an unknown Chinese woman would have such compassion for her when she knew she had absolutely nothing to gain from doing so. Again it reminded her of God's care and provision for them in so many wonderful ways.

Years later Ken and Maybeth learned that Mr. Maag was arrested the next day by the Japanese. Because he had helped Canadians, he was tied to a pole and beaten and finally released to continue with his missionary work there. Even with all he suffered, he would have said, "I'll do it again."

The cart finally came along and the coolie took an hour's rest sleeping underneath the cart. Eventually, however, Ken woke Maybeth, knowing they had to continue. Maybeth felt so much more rested from the harrowing bicycle ride because of that hour or so of sleep. They continued until nightfall, found a place to spend the night and the next morning they found themselves near the large city, Lishui. In Lishui the airfield held by Chinese Nationalist troops, was bracing for imminent bombing by the Japanese. Ken and Maybeth had spent the morning cycling, stopping and waiting for the cart, and then cycling some more. Around noon they arrived at the edge of the city and just as they approached the airfield, Japanese planes flew over and started to bomb the airfield.

Ken stopped, looked at Maybeth and said, "You know, I couldn't even care about the bombs; I'm too tired. Let's lie down here in the ditch until it is over."

So they lay down in the ditch right beside the airfield; the coolie pulling the cart found some gravestones on a nearby hillside to hide behind. Ken and Maybeth no sooner lay down in that ditch than they fell asleep and stayed fast asleep while the airplanes bombed the airfield close beside them. Weariness and trust in their faithful God had overcome their fears.

When the bombing was over they woke up, and Ken contacted another Swiss missionary friend to see if they could stay there for a bit to gather strength for further travel. Maybeth was getting terribly tired and could hardly keep upright on the bicycle. The missionary, Mr. Russangerber, thought that there was no safe haven for them in that city and, at considerable cost to himself, arranged for them to take a boat upstream and away from the Japanese advance. The boat owner had a boatful of wood to sell and was headed downstream to do so. Mr. Russangerber bought the entire load of wood, so that Ken could hire the empty boat to go back upstream.

Maybeth was very thankful for that boat. Ken rented the boat and paid off the carter who had carried their baggage and they headed upriver toward another mission station in Longquan.

When Ken arranged for the boatman to take them upriver, part of the arrangement was that he would provide meals. He did, but all he had was cabbage and fat pork. Ken and Maybeth were several days on the boat; Maybeth's pregnancy left her so exhausted that she felt rather sick. Day after day, three meals a day, they were served fat pork and boiled cabbage. Normally Maybeth wouldn't have minded at all, but she was feeling nauseous anyway and every day, breakfast, lunch, and dinner all she smelled was very greasy fat pork. She could hardly stand to put it in her mouth.

At night, the boatman would pull over to the bank and they would all sleep, the boatman, Ken and Maybeth, with a quilt pulled over them.

A few days of resting in the boat, and eating cabbage and fat pork however, were enough, and their sore muscles stiffened up and ached. Soon they were thinking of how much faster they could travel by bicycle. Maybeth had friends, the Keils, a German couple, in Yunhe, just over half the way to Longquan, and she and Ken thought that a bicycle trip to their home would be a good break. The problem, however, was what to do with the boat and the luggage. As they were puzzling over this problem, they saw some Roman Catholic priests on the bank hailing them. When they approached, one of the fathers said that his companion was very sick and asked if they could share the boat to get him to medical help. Ken quickly arranged for them to use the boat and to continue the journey with Ken and Maybeth's luggage, heading for Longquan. Ken and Maybeth cycled to Yunhe and thoroughly enjoyed four restful days with the Keils. What a privilege it was to have such good German friends where they could enjoy relative security and comfort.

They arrived in Yunhe on Tuesday night and Ken felt they should leave on Friday morning. The Keils cycled with them for a short distance and it was hard to say "goodbye" not knowing when they would ever see them again. The world at war and China in such a state of flux generally meant that they would not see dear friends for a very long time if ever.

They cycled for the rest of the day after leaving the Keils and toward dark it began to rain. Although it was only thirty miles from Yunhe to Longquan, the road was over mountainous territory on a narrow road with switchbacks and the bicycling was slow going. They stopped in a filthy inn for the night. Trying to sleep amid pigs and fleas and other flying insects as well as rowdy crowds in the inn was barely possible, even for Maybeth who could sleep anywhere, so by morning they felt that they had hardly slept at all.

Weary again, the next morning they headed out early, but by eight o'clock it was raining. Ken did have an umbrella, and they took turns holding the umbrella over their heads as they cycled side by side down the road. The Chinese looked at them and shook their heads at the ridiculous sight. They still got very wet and finally were soaked through and chilled, so Ken looked for shelter. Just ahead in the road was a tiny temple, a very cheap sort of affair with a covered portion at the back where the idol was kept and an open area in front. There was an enclosed courtyard, but the majority of it had no roof. When they entered they found that there was some straw on the ground. Apparently a beggar sleeping there had dragged in some straw to sleep on. Ken knew that they had to get their clothes dry and so since there was no one anywhere around, he decided that they should take their outer clothes off, start a fire with the little pile of straw, and dry themselves and their clothes at the fire. They did with Ken periodically checking the road to make sure there were no travelers coming.

Finally after standing by the fire in their underwear and holding their clothes over the fire, they were fairly dry. They put on their dry clothes again when the rain stopped, and returned to the road.

The highway was truly scenic; it wended its way through mountain canyons with hundreds of waterfalls along the way. Ken wrote,

The road went through the most wonderful scenery we had yet seen in China. Verdant foliage, thickly forested mountains, and hills from which came down hundreds of cataracts. Sometimes we would round a corner in the road and be confronted with a huge waterfall coming right down from a cliff and splashing over the road. On this road it was not difficult to get water which was safe to drink for most of the district was uninhabited and the water came right down the sheer cliff from rocky springs way up on the mountain.

It was steep, though, and Maybeth, already tired from lack of sleep and weeks of travel, quickly tired on the hills. Ken tied a piece of rope from the back of the seat of his bicycle to the handlebars of hers and pedaled furiously. Maybeth rode along behind and simply kept balance. It looked like a bicycle built for two, except that Ken was doing most of the work pulling them up the mountainsides.

That night they arrived in a city where there was a mission station manned by a German couple whom Ken and Maybeth did not know well. They stayed there for a day or two until their luggage arrived by boat. The couple was very welcoming, but Ken quickly noticed a picture of the woman's brother dressed in Gestapo uniform hanging on the wall, and written on the bottom of the photo were the words "Heil Hitler. God punish England." Ken had known that this couple was quite pro Hitler at this time, before they learned of all the atrocities he had done. Ken and Maybeth were amused at the irony of Canadian citizens, living in their home, enjoying good camaraderie and hospitality, but being very careful to stay off the subject of politics.

When their luggage arrived Ken made arrangements to go on to Longquan which had an empty mission station and where they could live for awhile. How they hoped that they could stay there in one place for a reasonable length of time!

Chapter Twenty-one

They had what they needed to live there in the mission home in Longquan, but, lacking a radio, they missed knowing what was going on in the world. Across the city was a Roman Catholic compound occupied by a group of priests. Often in the evening Ken and Maybeth would cycle across the city to visit them and hear the evening news from the United States. They became fond of these priests, but found their approach to their work amusing. They would sit around playing cards in undershirts and old pants by the hour. Then suddenly, right in the middle of a rousing card game, one of them would jump up and exclaim, "Oh my God; it's time for Mass." They would all leap to their feet, take their priestly habits from pegs on the walls of the room, and rush out and say Mass for those Chinese who had gathered. Then they'd come back and fling their gowns back on the pegs and resume their card game. This pattern seemed to be the daily schedule. They said Mass several times a day and the rest of the time they played cards and listened to world news.

Inevitably the news carried threats of further Japanese incursion. During the month they stayed in Longquan, the airfield at Lishui, about 75 miles away fell into Japanese hands and, unwilling to risk another sudden flight, Ken and Maybeth decided to move on again. The banks and businesses in Longquan were moving, not wanting to risk falling into Japanese hands. It was difficult to find transportation. When the Japanese advanced, the populations of the cities in their path fled toward free China. That meant that all bus, train, or boat transportation was crammed full and many were forced to walk. Refugees flooded the highways and waterways, running ahead of the Japanese army. The flood of refugees became part of the landscape and certainly complicated travel.

Fleeing the Japanese advance, entire factories moved with coolies carrying machinery and inventory west and south. Schools and universities moved with professors organizing the westward march, creating groups to lead, groups to bring up the rear, groups to care for the sick, and groups to forage for food and shelter. At times the roads were so crowded one walked elbow to elbow with the hurrying, swarming crowd.

Undeterred by the circumstances of political upheaval, floods, steaming hot weather, cold rain, and frequent bombing, the refugee river flowed onward, surmounting disasters and unbelievable hardships. Shoes wore out and were patched or discarded. Refugees contracted dysentery and cholera from drinking impure water out of necessity. The oldest and youngest became ill and often died along the way.

They traveled by every method of transportation imaginable: small flat bottomed boats on the rivers and canals, bicycles, rickshaws, but mostly on foot, carrying their most precious household goods on their backs. Children tried to keep up and when exhausted were often carried in baskets on shoulders of parents and grandparents.

Always moving, the river of humanity trudged toward free land, away from the atrocities of the Japanese occupation of their cities. Cities were emptied ahead of the Japanese. Night and day the river of humanity moved on.

This time Ken and Maybeth planned to travel to Fukien province which had no China Inland Mission work. Ken had heard of a group of missionaries who were in Puch'eng without funds, and, as local secretary, he withdrew a sum of money and headed for Puch'eng. Of course, with the multitudes of refugees, there were no carts, no trains, and no transportation to be found. Once again, their God provided just as they were giving up the search. Quite unexpectedly, the Salt Gabelle, a European company in China, offered them a ride in one of their trucks, and the chance to take all their baggage with them. "We with our nine pieces of luggage seemed rich and increased with goods compared to the missionaries in Puch'eng who had fled with nothing more than a suitcase or two," Ken commented. The truck was carrying drums of gasoline and Ken and Maybeth sat in the back with the gasoline and their meager belongings. In one place on the road there had been a tremendous landslide and they had to disembark. They imagined all their luggage, along with the truck, sliding over the edge of the road and down the cliff, but with careful driving the truck was able to negotiate the road. Then about 20 miles from Puch'eng, the truck broke down and could go no further. Glad to have found transportation that far, Ken and Maybeth left their baggage on the truck, got off, and cycled to Puch'eng, arriving late in the afternoon.

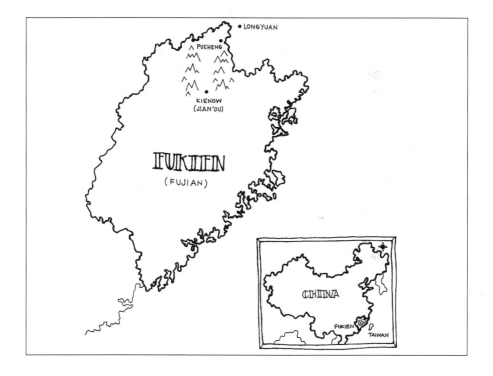

Fukien Province.

They arrived at the mission station run by two old Anglican ladies from another mission society who insisted that they stay. Gathered in that house were 15 missionaries, 13 of them refugees like themselves from all over west Zhejiang. Nine were China Inland Mission and the other 4 were Baptist missionaries from Kinhwa. One of them was John Davis, an old friend from Yongkang, the one they called John, the Baptist. These 13 missionaries had experienced a terrible trip from their stations, all of them losing practically everything they possessed. Some of the ladies had only two dresses and no winter clothing at all. They had walked miles and miles over hilly roads with nothing to eat except rice porridge with no milk or even salt to improve the taste, and not a drop of water to drink at times. At least four of them were over 60 years old and had made the journey on foot. Some of the younger workers had bicycles, but they were so laden with baggage that they were hard pressed to ride and had pushed the bicycles most of the way. After many days of traveling in this manner, all had arrived at Puch'eng in a state of almost complete exhaustion and near collapse. Some had been confined immediately to bed and were barely able to eat although they were starving hungry and had lost considerable weight.

Many of them had incredible stories to tell of escape from the encroaching Japanese. Two ladies had traveled from Chuhsien on a truck full of hand grenades that the Chinese army wanted to remove from the city before the Japanese came. Of course, the fear of a pin slipping out or of someone shooting the truck was constant. On top of those dangers, there were bombs that had been discarded from the retreat of the Chinese army, lying armed along the side of the road. If the Japanese chose to strafe the road, as they so often did, sudden death would have been the result. The two ladies at the station, over 60 themselves, had taken in all these refugees, welcoming them and caring for them selflessly.

The house was a large, rambling building, and the wide verandahs were filled with beds since there were not enough rooms, making it look like a school dormitory. Everyone crowded up to two big tables for meals. It was such a happy crowd, everyone laughing and full of praise to God. An onlooker would never know from their talk and faces that they had lost everything they possessed and had no homes and absolutely no plans for the future except to move on again if the Japanese came closer! They sang grace at meals and every morning at 10:30, they

146

would read the Bible together. It was almost like a convention there in war torn China!

All the guests helped the two old ladies in charge, but they kept on declaring they hadn't had such a good time in their lives before with such a big happy family of Christian folks! Food was scarce and they had to scrounge to buy eggs and, in fact, any food. Each morning someone would go out into the city to try to buy vegetables. Ken and another missionary went out on bicycles into the country and would buy eggs one at a time from anyone who had one to sell. Sometimes they were able to buy a chicken and everyone ate well that day. It was no small task to provide enough food for this family of almost twenty.

Puch'eng was bombed very frequently and Ken and Maybeth went out walking after the bombing to see which places had survived and which ones had not. They also tried to determine what places in buildings were the safest when the bombs hit. They looked at houses that had been bombed, noting what part of the house still stood and what parts fell and soon concluded that the parts of the houses that seemed most reliable were the corners. The vibration and spray of shrapnel were lessened where there were two walls to support one another. Another place which seemed to be safe was under a kitchen table. Many Chinese would hide under the table, sometimes throwing a quilt over the table first. Flying debris caused many injuries, and sometimes fighter planes would follow the bombers and strafe the streets with machine guns as the citizens fled the devastation.

After analysis, each of the missionaries determined a place of safety when the bombers came and the alarm rang. As they had seen in other cities, the air raid alarm was the local temple bell. When the planes were in the large regional area, the bells would ring out slowly. If the planes were nearer and seemed to be coming in their direction, the bell would ring double time. If the planes were approaching the city and there was imminent danger, the bells would ring madly announcing the urgency of the situation.

When the first alarms rang, most of the missionaries would note them, but keep doing their tasks. Then as the alarms became more urgent, they all retired to the part of the house they thought the safest. There were usually a couple ladies sitting under the stairs, some standing in the corners and some under the kitchen table. The two Anglican ladies always went to a little dugout in their back garden, a flimsy little dugout that seemed so frail that Ken was convinced an errant rock could have gone through the roof. They, however, had unswerving confidence in the dugout. John Davis was as thin as a rail. He was around six foot three and weighed only about one hundred and thirty-five pounds. Ken and Maybeth used to laugh at him because when the alarm went off, he got right out of the house, went into the garden and stood behind a palm tree. As the planes moved around the city, he would move around the tree, keeping it between him and the bombing. Mrs. Davis was very heavy and never felt like doing anything when the planes came. So she would just stay in her room sitting in her rocking chair. It didn't matter how urgent the alarm was, no one was moving her out of her rocker.

Ken and Maybeth were amused watching the differing attitudes and convictions of safety in regard to the bombers. After the planes left, they would all come out of their separate hiding places, meet together, and thank the Lord for protecting them. Then they would go out into the city to help those who had not been as fortunate. One of Ken's sayings at that time was, "Not a single shaft can hit, till the Son of God sees fit." That didn't mean that they shouldn't try to protect themselves, but both Ken and Maybeth knew that if God wanted to take them now that they would be ready. But if God still had a ministry for them to do, then no bombing in the world could touch them.

Ken and Maybeth remained in Puch'eng for a couple months and enjoyed the companionship of the other missionaries. One morning a Chinese Christian man came to the house and said, "I hear that there are some China Inland Mission missionaries here in this home."

Maybeth said that there were.

He continued, "I was led to God by a CIM missionary in a distant city and we now have a group of Christians here in Puch'eng who worship God. We realize that you missionaries have had a hard time and have had to be refugees, leaving your homes and many of you losing everything you possessed. Our group has taken up an offering and we would like you to take it and divide it up among your missionaries."

Maybeth was very touched. In the early days of missionary work in China, it was always the missionaries who would help with medical help and monetary help as the church struggled to establish itself. In fact, many new Chinese Christians looked to the missionary for financial help. Now, it appeared, the tide had turned and the Chinese were giving to the missionaries out of gratitude and out of recognition that the needs of the missionary were greater than theirs. It was a real example of Christian love and the little group there in Puch'eng was so grateful and so moved by it.

After Ken and Maybeth had lived a few months in Puch'eng, the consensus of the group there was that because Maybeth was pregnant and wouldn't be able to ride a bicycle much longer, they should go further west, away from Japanese-occupied territory. No one wanted this baby to arrive while there was danger of the Japanese invading the city. So they started out on two bikes again, having sent luggage ahead with a coolie. Although cycling presented its problems, Maybeth had learned to ride a bike well. Her bike had no brakes and neither did Ken's, so they would put one foot on the front wheel when they wanted to slow down. This maneuver became difficult when seven or eight months pregnant and it had a tendency to throw the rider off balance. Once Maybeth managed to stop the bicycle, she would slide it sideways since there wasn't a chance she could lift her foot over the bar on the man's bike.

CHAPTER TWENTY-TWO

They traveled south more than 60 miles in the fall of 1942 through Fukien province until they came to the city of Kienow where there was a Commonwealth Missionary Society mission station (Church of England missionaries). The mission station was run by an archdeacon of the Anglican Church who was a lot of fun and not at all as stuffy as his title suggested. He referred to himself as the "arch demon."

Most importantly, however, there was a doctor there. After taking a look at Maybeth, the doctor said to Ken, "You realize that you are going to have a delivery if you keep on traveling like this. Would you like for me to give you instructions of what to do in the case of a delivery?"

Ken said, "No sweat, I'm a diary farmer."

Maybeth secretly thought he was a bit nervous about the delivery never having seen a human baby born. Gwen was born in the hospital in Ningbo and Ken had not been there when she was delivered. The doctor gave Ken a little bag of sterilized bandages and other necessities for a delivery.

They were glad to have the doctor check them out. He pronounced them both healthy, although Ken weighed only about 134 pounds and obviously had been under a great deal of stress in the last year. Not only was he anxious about the birth of the child, he was also concerned about the Japanese advance and on top of it all, he had taken the extra assigned duties of local secretary of the CIM. In that capacity his duties included getting monthly stipends to missionaries who at times were fleeing the Japanese as he was. Trying to hit moving targets made him anxious, since he knew that the missionaries were counting on their monthly allowance for food and travel. In time, the stress began to take a toll and Ken began to suffer from abdominal pain. He brushed it aside as something he had no time to deal with and continued his work.

There was never a doubt that Ken and Maybeth would have to continue their journey since Kienow was certainly not a safe haven from the Japanese. Their missionary friends there had heard about several buses that had come from the plains of northern Kiangsi, where they had run a regular bus route. The owners were taking these buses down through the province of Fukien to southern Kiangsi. The bus owners feared the Japanese advances, and felt that if they wanted to keep these buses, they would need to take them over the mountains into southern Kiangsi. They planned to drive them through southern Fukien and then across the mountainous terrain into southern Kiangsi, where it was hoped someone might want to buy them. The missionaries in Kienow were acquainted with the bus drivers and asked them if they would take Ken and Maybeth and a few other Chinese when they went. Although the head driver was reluctant and said that he had not intended to take passengers, he agreed to take them. So the four buses were to go across the flat plains of southern Fukien and then across the mountainous roads into southern Kiangsi. Ken wanted to go to Kanhsien in southern Kiangsi and thought that the provision of the buses was a wonderful solution.

The bus drivers clearly explained to them that, in the interest of safety, the four buses were always going to travel together and if one broke down all four would wait while that bus was being repaired. The drivers were concerned that Ken and Maybeth would object to the delay while repairs were made. They warned Ken that the buses were not in good repair, and the chance of delay was almost sure. He assured them that they wouldn't mind. Any transportation was better than riding bicycles, they thought. Ken 's abdominal pain had worsened, and he dreaded causing Maybeth to deliver early with more bicycle riding. His ability to help Maybeth over hills on their bicycles was going to be limited if the pain continued and he thought the buses would be a carefree way to travel.

The buses were most certainly not in good repair. Ken and Maybeth sat at the front beside the side door of one of them. The door latch was either in need of repair or nonexistent and so a piece of cloth was tied to the door and fastened to the back of one of the seats to hold the door shut. The window where the cloth was tied was either permanently down or broken.

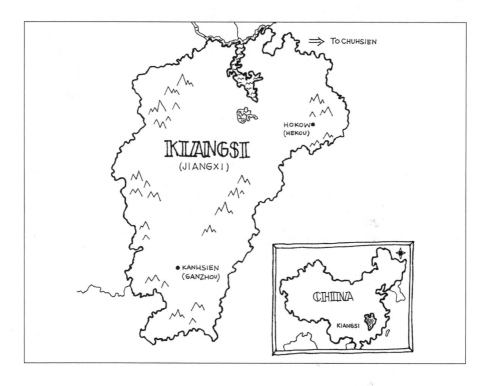

Kiangsi province (now named Jiangxi province.

Soon after they started, they quickly began to see that the trip could prove dangerous. A huge problem soon became apparent: the bus drivers had no idea how to drive a manual transmission vehicle on hills. As long as they were traveling on relatively flat country, the buses went along smoothly. The men had driven only on a small area of level plains of northern Kiangsi, and before long as they approached the borders of Fukien, they were facing hilly and eventually mountainous country. The road over the mountains included hairpin bends and wound along the edge of sheer cliffs with steep hillsides above and below it. The drivers had never learned how to shift down a gear or two when necessary. In fact, they apparently did not know that shifting down was an option.

To add to these problems, the buses, which were designed to run on gasoline or diesel, were running on burning charcoal. Common wisdom held that the Chinese could ruin a vehicle quicker than anyone else on earth. Then after they had ruined it, they could keep it running longer than anyone else on earth.

The drivers, who were also the mechanics, had added conversion kits to enable the buses to run on charcoal and the extra equipment hung on the side of the bus with steam pouring out as the bus sputtered its way down the road. Sometimes in the morning the buses were hard to start, apparently a common problem with charcoal burning vehicles. The solution was to take out the spark plugs and put them in the charcoal fire, heat them up, take them out with tongs and put them back into the engine. It worked almost all the time, with the bus engine roaring to life. Ken and Maybeth would put their boxes on the bus, take their seats and sit tight, white-knuckled all the way.

When the buses in the caravan approached the hills, however, the ride became hair-raising. The hapless drivers would start up the hill, never thinking when the bus slowed down that they must change gears. Up the hill they would go; the engine would start to lug until finally it would begin to chug and sputter and finally stall. Of course at this point, the bus would start to roll back down the hill. To add drama to the situation, the brakes were very poor, but a plan had been devised for that eventuality. A young man sat near the back door of the bus with two triangular pieces of wood. Whenever the bus started to roll backwards and the brakes wouldn't hold, the fellow would jump out and put the blocks behind the back wheels. Then began the business of starting the engine again.

When it was successfully started and the bus was moving in first gear, the designated fellow would pick up the blocks, throw them in the bus and leap in himself as the bus crawled up the hill. As soon as they came to a more level spot, the driver would shift into second and third and they would move along nicely until they came to a hill or a switchback and then the engine would lug down, sputter and die, the blocks would be placed and the engine started again. No matter how many times they went through this scenario, the drivers never caught on to the idea of gearing down on hills and sharp turns.

Ken and Maybeth were more than anxious. Every time the bus started to roll backwards, they quickly untied the knot on the piece of cloth holding the door, and jumped out. They would then stand on the edge of the road looking over the cliff they might have rolled over, watch the blocks being put behind the wheels and the starting of the bus and climb back in again. After a few of these escapades they took a look at the hill, and despite the discomfort that Ken suffered, concluded that it wasn't that steep, and tell the driver that they would meet him at the top. They both felt much better walking up the hill. It eliminated the fear of rolling backwards over the cliff on the steep and mountainous roads.

Going downhill was just about as bad. The brakes were practically worthless, and whenever the bus approached a switchback, Ken and Maybeth could imagine their bus not negotiating the bend and going right over the side of the road and down the mountain. At one place they saw a bus turned over at the bottom of a cliff, and in another a military truck sliding off the side of the road precariously near the sheer precipice. Somehow the planned restful bus trip became more stressful than the physical hardship of riding bicycles over the mountains.

For a while the buses would go along a stretch that was fairly level and Ken and Maybeth began to think they would make good time but as soon as they gained confidence, one of the four buses would break down, sputtering and stopping. All the buses stopped and all four drivers and extra helpers converged on the broken-down bus and conferred about what to do to get it going again. They would tinker with the bus engine for interminable lengths of time. Sometimes they tinkered with it for an hour and got it going; other times it would take all day to fetch parts and fashion repairs. So the trip, which should have been no more than one day, took several days.

Ken and Maybeth determined that they were not going to allow their exasperation with the trip to make them sour and disgusted, so they found a way to entertain themselves while they waited for the bus to be repaired and continue on.

Ken found a piece of cardboard and drew squares on it with charcoal. Then when he and Maybeth got out of the bus for a repair stop, they would pick up stones at the side of the road and play checkers. The Chinese passengers who were traveling with them were amused at their checker games, calm demeanor and lack of frustration, frustration that the rest of the travelers were certainly feeling.

Once when they had been told that the stop would take all day, they walked to a nearby river, found a secluded spot, hung their clothes on the bushes and with soap in hand bathed their dirty, dusty bodies in the river. It was a refreshing luxury after days of sitting on that sooty, charcoal-burning bus. Sometimes at night sleeping was difficult. The buses stopped at the end of the day and the drivers and passengers found their own accommodations. One night they slept on the hard stone floor of a temple in front of the temple idol. Another night they slept on a low kitchen table in a Chinese home. The homeowners had no more beds; Ken and Maybeth were just two more in a long string of refugees and so the best they could offer was the table. There were people under the table also. As they passed through villages, Ken and Maybeth would pick up a little bit of food as they could find it, glad that they had acquired a taste for Chinese food.

One evening, when they had been told the buses wouldn't go until half way through the next day, they discovered that there was a missionary in the village. They walked up to the home of a couple with the American Methodist Missionary society and introduced themselves. These Methodist missionaries gladly took them in and they were able to bathe, wash a few clothes, wash their hair, and were renewed by the kindness and good fellowship they enjoyed. The following day they finally made it into Kanhsien and the mission station where they hoped to have the baby.

CHAPTER TWENTY-THREE

When they arrived in Kanhsien they were reunited with good friends, the Tylers. Vera Tyler was expecting a baby. Also at that mission station were friends, the Faulkners. Cyril was Australian and his wife was American and they had just delivered their first baby, Margie. Nearby was Grace Emblem, the maternity nurse for the province, who had already been on hand to deliver the Faulkner's Margie. Maybeth's baby was due in less than a month and the Tyler baby was due a month or so after that. So the Mission leaders suggested that Grace stay in Kanhsien for the deliveries. There was also a Scottish doctor who was just leaving Kanhsien when Ken and Maybeth arrived. He said that if he were still there, he would deliver the baby, but if he were gone they should ask an Austrian doctor, a Dr. Fritz Yensen, who lived just outside the city, and he would probably come and help.

Dr. Yensen had left Vienna because of his Jewish blood and like George Sgalitzer, the doctor who had delivered Gwen, was waiting out the war working in China. His first stop after leaving Vienna was to lend his assistance in the Spanish Civil War and now he had moved on to this war in China. He was a gifted surgeon and able to improvise when necessary. He was very different than Sgalitzer, though, in that he lacked the graciousness and old world charm of Dr. Sgalitzer. Yensen was abrupt and seemed callous in his dealings until Ken and Maybeth got to know him. Then they quickly grew accustomed to his manner and became very fond of him.

Ken's abdominal pain had not decreased on the trip from Puch'eng to Kanhsien. He didn't know what might have caused the pain. He thought that he might even be suffering from appendicitis. The pains were intermittent and often very painful. When the Scottish doctor examined him, he diagnosed the problem as appendicitis, but he was leaving immediately and suggested that we consult with Dr. Yensen. Yensen was hesitant to diagnose the problem as appendicitis but couldn't determine what else it could be. He and Ken decided to take out his appendix as a start. The Catholic compound in Kanhsien had a small hospital and an operating theater. At the kind invitation of the sisters in the hospital, it was arranged that Ken would have surgery there. Any facilities the hospital had would be at the doctor's disposal.

Before the operation, Ken discussed with the doctor his intellectual interest in his own body, saying, "You know, I always wondered what an appendix looks like. Will you save mine when you take it out and let me see what it looks like?"

The doctor agreed. When he was opened up, however, and the appendix removed, the doctor along with some other practitioners at the hospital found nodules on Ken's intestines and their diagnosis was that he had some strain of intestinal TB. Their recommendation was that Ken have enforced rest for about 6 months so that his body could recover, something he and Maybeth thought might be almost impossible with the arrival of a baby any day. The doctor explained that this intestinal problem was apparently a disease his body had previously contracted but that it had been dormant until the stress of their recent lifestyle; they had been too exhausted, too stressed, had been eating whatever came to hand, and going without enough sleep. Ken's anxiety over getting Maybeth to a place of safety and the constant fear of being overrun by the Japanese had caused the dormant disease to manifest itself. They also attributed the source of the infection to Ken's life on the dairy farm as a boy where his family had a herd of cows that were later destroyed because the milk had tested positive for TB. Before the herd was destroyed, however, Ken and his brothers had drunk that milk daily.

The sisters who ran the hospital were wonderful to them, attentive to their every need. After the operation Ken asked about the appendix. The doctor told him that he had wrapped it up in a piece of gauze and the next morning had found the gauze at the top of a rat hole. His only assumption had been that his appendix had been eaten. The rats devouring his appendix was fodder for jokes for many months following the surgery.

As Ken recuperated, he frequently walked down the hall to the chapel where there was an organ, and the sisters who had cared for him came down and knelt and meditated as Ken played. He played great old hymns of the church such as " A Mighty Fortress is Our God." a professed favorite of many of the sisters. Ken chose not to make the point about its author being Martin Luther.

Ken recuperated slowly and was very weak after the operation. He wrote often to his dear friend, Lem Fowler and in one letter he confessed to Lem,

We miss our wee Gwen terribly at times, but I think I can say that if God gave us the chance to have her back again we would not want to take her from her service in the King's Court and bring her back to this wicked world. She is happy and has not shed a tear since the ones we wiped from her eyes after she breathed her last breath... and never shall [weep] again. We shall go to her and the union shall indeed be a joyous one. I think that my little girlie shall run with a jump into my arms when I cross over to that side. Had it not been for Maybeth, I think I should have actually wanted to go when I had this operation and was so weak, but I could not bear the thought of Maybeth alone.

Their dear friend, Vera Tyler, said of Ken and Maybeth at the time that their feelings were "raw" after losing Gwen. It was a time to stop running from the Japanese for a short while, but also a place where they could take the time to grieve for the loss of their dear little girl.

Kanhsien was a large city and there was good food available, such things Ken and Maybeth had not seen for a very long time: good milk and beef and fresh vegetables. However, during the years 1942 and 1943 when they were there, inflation was rampant. A typewriter ribbon cost $200-$500 and Ken had to have several pair of shoes half-soled for $290 a pair, a better choice than buying new shoes at up to $450 a pair. A great portion of the allowance sent by the CIM went for food and everything else had to be mended or done without. It was neither the first time nor the last that Ken and Maybeth would have to do without many of the necessities of ordinary life. And yet, they were grateful for the faithfulness of their Lord in supplying their every need.

There was a good-sized Christian community in Kanhsien, including a Christian Middle School (corresponding to an American high school). Some of these students and their principal had come south from Shanghai for safety from the Japanese advance. During the coldest part of 1941, the principal and his younger brother left Shanghai and came through Japanese lines to safety in Free China, bringing the students from the Christian school in Shanghai with him. They suffered a terrible year, seeing many of the students die along the road, suffering sickness themselves, seeing their students sick, and finding no means of support. This principal was very anxious over the state of these young folk, many of whom were miles and miles from their homes. His greatest concern was for their spiritual welfare and he would daily exhort them to bear witness to the Lord's provision for them. During the Chinese New Year celebration in Kanhsien many of these same young students were out on the streets helping others in need and telling the good news of the Gospel of Christ. Ken and Maybeth were encouraged by the practical Christianity displayed by these children and so many of the Christians in Kanhsien.

They had planned that the baby would be born at home and so to prepare for that day, they raised a bed so that it would be easier to have help delivering the baby if that should be necessary. Dr. Yensen agreed to help out and said to call him when they thought the baby was coming. He lived on the outskirts of the city, outside the city walls. Rumor had it that he had several Chinese women who lived with him and that he was no moral giant. Ken and Maybeth loved him, however, and Ken spent many hours building a solid relationship with him. Grace Emblem, the missionary nurse was in the mission station also, in preparation for the baby's arrival.

Finally one night it was apparent that the baby was coming and, since Ken was still too weak to do much cycling, he asked Bill Tyler to go out to the city gates and try to contact the doctor. When Bill got to the city gates, great metal gates with prongs that extended to the ground, they were closed. Bill had to squeeze under the gates in the muddy road, find the doctor and bring him back to the mission compound, both of them squeezing under the city gate. Yensen arrived just as he had been found in the middle of the night, dressed in black silk pajamas embroidered with a huge red dragon on the front. His hair was shaggy, very curly, and stood up on end. He made a memorable vision that night when he arrived to deliver the baby; black curly hair standing straight up, a good growth of whiskers and the silk pajamas with a red dragon spitting fire across his chest.

That night, October 29, 1942, Donald Ian arrived. Besides the flashily dressed doctor, Grace Emblem also helped with what turned out to be an easy birth. Miss Emblem was a dear lady but quite fussy and able to always say the wrong thing at the wrong time. She fussed because the baby was a boy and she didn't like boy babies, because they might soak her when she changed their diapers. The day following the birth she told Maybeth that she was doing well, but she said, "You never can tell. I knew a family that lost their mother a week after she delivered!" What a story to tell a new mother! But Maybeth knew she never would have intentionally hurt anyone and so her words were not a problem.

Ian was a healthy baby, and Maybeth had plenty of milk, so he thrived. Yensen came to visit quite often. He never charged Ken and Maybeth for helping with the delivery, but only asked that Maybeth bake him some cookies now and then. She took it upon herself to mend his clothes also when she saw the need. He was living strictly Chinese and never saw the baked goods that the missionaries sometimes made.

Sometimes Yensen would come for supper to the mission station where the three couples were living and regale them all with stories of his youth. It seemed that he was from a poor family in Vienna, but determined early to become a doctor. To fund his education he used a skill he had learned as a boy, the art of jujitsu. He was a master in that martial art and found work teaching the Vienna police the techniques of jujitsu. He thought of himself as an athlete and carried a small javelin with him. On the porch outside their room, where Ken would often sit as he recuperated was a wooden divider with knotholes in it. Yensen would stand at one end of the porch and throw the javelin through whatever knothole he had designated beforehand. Although he was certainly not Christian, Ken and Maybeth loved him dearly and knew that he would have done anything for them had they asked.

The bombing of the city continued. Ian was only an hour old when bombers flew over the city and Maybeth hurriedly put him under the bed to ensure that he wouldn't be injured with flying debris. They did not fear Japanese invasion, however, and were used to living in cities that were the targets of bombs.

After 6 months of relatively quiet recuperation, the doctor determined that Ken needed another 6 months of quiet rest, so the little family remained in that mission station with the Tylers and the Faulkners for the fall of 1942 and into the spring of 1943. Ken read a great deal, wrote letters, and helped with the household duties. He was a marvelous cook, having been raised by an invalid mother in a houseful of boys. As the youngest, he had learned to cook well. Although the Faulkners were in charge of the mission station there in Kanhsien, Mrs. Faulkner was a cook with little interest in gourmet cooking. One day she would buy liver and boil it for hours and the three families would have liver soup. Then the next day they'd have the grayish colored, flavorless, boiled-out, tough-as-nails, liver. As a side dish they were served purple cabbage. Although hardly fussy about food, Maybeth couldn't think of anything much worse than a plate of gray liver and purple cabbage. Mrs. Faulkner didn't have any idea of making anything look appetizing and she was unfamiliar with Chinese products. Ken eased his way into the kitchen and soon the meals improved.

About a month after Ian was born, Vera Tyler gave birth to Gordon. Vera had a tough delivery and developed pleurisy after the birth. She could not seem to shake the infection and was weak with very little appetite. Since meals were unappetizing to begin with, and Vera had so little desire to eat, Ken and Maybeth were very concerned about her. She continued to lose weight and their anxiety grew. One day Ken suggested to Mrs. Faulkner that he take over cooking, only for Vera. She was in agreement. Ken walked to the shopping district and bought a Chinese green vegetable that tasted just like celery and a fresh fish. Kanhsien was on a river and fish was very available and reasonable. He baked the fish with a little ginger and celery and offered it to Vera. She was thrilled and thought the food tasted so good. She began to eat the food that Ken made for her and gradually her strength returned. One day he told her he was going to make cinnamon rolls for her. There was no cinnamon to be found in the city, but Ken went to the medicine shop and brought home a kashir bud that tasted much like cinnamon and, mixed with brown sugar, available anywhere, and Chinese yeast, he made wonderful cinnamon rolls. Ken was always ready to try Chinese products and of course those were the cheapest to buy. His interest in food and cooking was another gift of God.

As inflation affected the country, the China Inland Mission determined that it was only right to use the exchange rate set by the government. There were many places to exchange money on the black market that would give much more for American dollars, but the Mission felt that adhering to the national laws was an important stand to make. As a result, American dollars would exchange at a rate of 1 to 15 at the government exchange offices, but because dollars were in such high demand, businesses in the towns could exchange them on the black market at a rate of about 1 to 80. This meant that money sent from America suffered in the exchange and CIM missionaries had barely enough to supply themselves with food.

That year, as Ken and Maybeth lived with the other two couples, even when they pooled their limited allowance there wasn't enough to buy more than the bare necessities. Constantly they were amazed at the way God provided for them. The CIM would not subtract from their allowance any special gifts sent to individuals since they believed that God would provide as He saw the need. Many times Ken and Maybeth would receive a gift just when they didn't know how they were going to live for the next week. One Chinese doctor in Kanhsien was concerned that they might not have enough protein and so supplied Maybeth and Vera, the two new mothers, with meat for an extended period of time. Ken's ability to buy food on the street and make it for all of them saved a lot of money as well as perking up appetites.

The Japanese continued to bomb the city frequently. Bombers would come straight across the city eight abreast and drop bombs all along the way. The two healthy men in the Mission compound, Bill and Cyril, built a bomb shelter in the back yard big enough for all six adults. They dug a deep trench, covered the top with planks and sandbags and old quilts to prevent shrapnel injuries. When the urgent air raid alarm went off, the mothers were the first to get in it. At no time during these bombing raids were the Japanese planes ever troubled with anti-aircraft fire or with Chinese fighters. There simply were no Chinese fighters or anti-aircraft guns available. The cities were easy targets, presenting no danger to Japanese bombers. The Chinese army consisted mostly of men and small arms fire. When the urgent alarm would ring the women would get into the bomb shelter with a child on each lap and the men would linger in the back yard looking for the bombers. When they got close, the men would come down into the dugout and all six adults would be safe in the shelter.

The city was not so protected, and after the raids Cyril and Bill would go out to help those who had become victims of the bombing. Ken was not well enough to help and suffered the frustration of staying in the house while the other men helped out the needy. Cyril and Bill carried the wounded to the hospital where they could find help. One time Bill Tyler was asked by a doctor to hold the leg of a fellow he had just brought in so that the doctor could work on it. Bill did so and soon found himself holding only a leg, a situation that caused him to pass out, hitting the floor. The doctor continued work as Bill lay in a faint on the floor. Maybeth found these times very exciting and in some instances frightening. And so they lived for the rest of that year.

That fall, 1943, the Japanese called a halt to much movement further inland. They were busily defending a large part of Southeast Asia that they had previously conquered, and the war in China was proving more difficult than anticipated. The Japanese had mistakenly believed that if they took the major cities, the rivers and railroads of China, the country would surrender. They did not count on the Chinese peasants' ability to endure. Chinese peasants had lived in poverty and bloodshed, in famine and flood, for centuries and a war caused little more hardship than they were already accustomed to. Many had fled the Japanese-held territory and were refugees, but a dogged determination on the part of Chiang-Kai Shek and his leaders would not countenance surrender. Not only was Chiang fighting the Japanese, he was also trying to hold down the Communist influence and hoping for more help from the United States.

In this time of relative quiet, however, the CIM thought that it was peaceful enough that Ken and Maybeth could go back into Zhejiang province to help with refugee work there. So that summer of 1843, Ken and Maybeth and one year old, Ian, traveled back up through Kiangsi province and into Zhejiang to the city of Chuhsien. (Quzhou).

PART FIVE - THE END OF THE JOURNEY

"The soul that on Jesus has leaned for repose,
I will not, I will not desert to his foes:
That soul, though all Hell should endeavor to shake,
I'll never, no never, no never forsake."

CHAPTER TWENTY-FOUR

Chuhsien was one of the cities that the Japanese chose to punish after Doolittle's raid. American bombers had taken off from an aircraft carrier in the Pacific, bombed the Japanese city of Kobe, and then flown on into Free China to land their airplanes. They had taken the Japanese almost completely by surprise with only minimal anti-aircraft defense in Japan. The bombing was carried out with extreme efficiency and accuracy. Since these bombers had departed from an aircraft carrier and didn't have enough fuel to return or the ability to land on the carrier, the arrangement with the Chinese Nationalist government had been to land at local airfields in China. Chuhsien was one of the cities where they planned to land. Since it was the middle of the night and the local area was in a blackout, the Chinese army officers were to put the lights on at the local airfield when they heard the planes arrive. It was said that the Chinese officers were gambling on a game of mahjong in the back room of the airport and perhaps drinking too, and so the lights were never put on.

However it happened, many pilots were stranded in the hills after crash landing their planes, and the Chinese brought them to Chuhsien where they were transported out to a safer area of China. Ken and Maybeth had met some of these young men in Yongkang after their raid and before they were flown down to Kunming and back to their bases. Because of the embarrassment of the Doolittle raid, the Japanese decided to make an example of Chuhsien, and as a result, there was hardly a building standing unharmed. Nevertheless, refugees had flooded into the city from surrounding bombed out cities. Because of the refugee problem in Chuhsien, Ken and Maybeth were asked to take over the administration of American relief funds.

169

Chuhsien was just on the border of no man's land and the Japanese were in Jinhua, the next big city. The city had been very peaceful of late and the Japanese seemed to be consolidating their gains and not attempting any recent drives. Perhaps the Japanese were sending extra men to the front in the South Pacific islands, leaving the countryside relatively quiet. Ken and Maybeth arrived in Chuhsien in 1943, when Ian was a year old, and stayed there for almost a year. Throughout that year they would frequently hear rumors that the Japanese were approaching and a sudden scare would ensue with many people packing up and planning to leave the city. Ken and Maybeth too, would pack up and make plans to leave. But then the rumors would die down when the Japanese didn't come.

Upon their arrival in Chuhsien, the Gray family found the city swarming with refugees. It was a pitiful, tragic sight. Many had lost everything they owned and were hopelessly sitting in the streets or on the sidewalks and huddling in corners where there was a little bit of shelter. The sound of children crying because they were hungry and cold was everywhere. Many needed clothing and food, so Ken and Maybeth set up rice kitchens where they would cook meals two or three times a week. Then, with the relief funds, they hired tailors to make the quilted clothing so prevalent in China for protection against the winter winds. The refugees were invited to come to the Mission compound to get a hot meal and clothing as it became available. The church in Chuhsien had been badly bombed and stood without a roof, but Ken began services there, and two or three times a week he and Maybeth distributed food and clothing for the refugees.

Because Ken and Maybeth wanted to feed the souls of these refugees as they gave them food, they arranged groups for telling them about the gospel of Jesus Christ. They divided the refugees into manageable sized groups; Ken would take the men, a young Chinese pastor would take the younger men, a young Chinese girl taught some of the younger women, and Maybeth took the old women. She soon found that these women had never had a day of education, never heard of Christ, and were devoted to their house idols and city idols. Maybeth's job was to teach them a Bible lesson and then after the lesson give them the rice and the clothing. The pathetic little group gathered in a corner of the bombed-out church with hardly any roof at all and sat, away from the wind and sometimes in the sunshine, on the ground. There Maybeth told them of Christ, a living, loving Savior who loved them, who heard their prayers and who cared about them personally, not like their idols. Every morning, Maybeth prayed for God's blessing and preached her heart out to these "old dears" as she called them, but there was never any response. All they would say was, "Is it time to get the food yet?" "Have you got a jacket for me?"

Discouraged, Maybeth talked with Ken. She understood that they were naturally concerned about their physical well being and hardly wanted to think about the love of God when they had been shown so little love as refugees. They thought that rice in the stomach was more important than a hope for eternal life. Ken and Maybeth prayed that the Holy Spirit would work in the hearts of these pathetic women and cause them to turn to Him.

One day as Maybeth sat with her old ladies, one of them said, "You know, you are trying so hard to teach us what it means to have your kind of religion, but you don't understand that we're different. You don't understand our circumstances. You're a white person; we're Chinese. You have all kinds of money; we don't have any. We're refugees and have lost everything; you don't know what it is to be in that situation."

"Just a minute," Maybeth said. "I do know what it is to be a refugee." And she told them a little bit about her past years, how often she had to run for her life just as they had. Often she and Ken had fled from the same cities they had left. They had run to the ditch to avoid the Japanese planes strafing the roads. They had hidden behind gravestones for shelter. They had gone hungry because there was no food. They had drunk water from off the hillsides, a sure way to contract cholera.

"I do know what it is to be a refugee," Maybeth told them.

"Ah," they said. "You do know what it means to be a refugee like us. But you've never lost your home and gone hungry and thirsty."

"Yes, I did." Maybeth answered. "We left our home with twenty

171

minutes preparation and the Japanese pursued us. We had to leave everything."

"That is interesting," they said. "But, you know, none of those things really matter. You can always find or get new things. You haven't lost a member of the family. Sometimes a child gets lost in a crowd and then we never see them again or one of them isn't strong and dies by the roadside. Then you have to bury them and never go back. You don't know what that is like."

And Maybeth said with tears in her eyes, "I do know that; it's just what we've been through." Then she told them a little bit about Gwen's death and how hard she had found it to be and yet God had comforted her heart. It was good to be able to pray to Him and He would give her the comfort and strength she needed.

"You're right," they slowly agreed. "We see now that you do know exactly how we feel. Now why don't you tell us about your God and what he has done for you?" That day some of the women lingered after the rest went off to get their meal and prayed with Maybeth and gave their lives to the service of that kind of God.

"It was only because we could identify with those people, know how they feel, and know their losses and their heartbreak, that they would listen," she told Ken after that meeting. Often, Maybeth thought, we Christians resent difficult times we have to go through and forget that we are being shaped into the image of Christ. One such purpose is to be able to minister to others who have suffered similarly. So she told Ken that sometimes she had thought that trials were sent to make them unhappy, but those trials have a divine purpose. Perhaps that purpose was to reach out a hand to those who suffered like they had but had no Savior to comfort them. Maybeth was reminded of Jack Sharman and his hand on Ken's shoulder after Gwen died. His comfort was more precious, because he had just gone through the same trial.

While they were in Chuhsien, Ian was growing up and entering his second year. Accordingly, he was a typical two-year-old, into every-thing. The church in Chuhsien gave Ken and Maybeth a welcome feast when they first arrived and it was their request that they bring the food into their house and serve it in their dining room. Their house had a wooden floor in the dining room, considered to be a luxury not found in many of the local homes, and so some tables were set up and the leaders of the local church came for a welcome feast where everyone could sit together and eat. It was typical of the people of that time to dispose of any food they didn't plan to eat by dropping it on the floor. Any bones or skin or other unwanted pieces found their way to the floor under the table. In their homes they were used to dirt floors where the pigs and chickens had free rein and would clean up anything that dropped. Dinner was usually accompanied by cackling hens and grunting pigs under the table. Ken and Maybeth made no sign that they even noticed the scraps going to the floor as they were determined not to embarrass these dear believers in any way. Maybeth had left Ian sleeping in a nearby bedroom and presumed that was where he still was. Imagine her surprise when one of the ladies touched her gently on the arm and pointed underneath the table. Ian had awakened and walked in unnoticed and was entertaining himself under the table putting everything into his mouth. Maybeth removed him from the room and tried vainly to pull everything out of his mouth that he had shoved into it, everything everyone else had spit out and discarded!

Before he turned two, Ian was playing in a room where there were some stored items, including Ken and Maybeth's bicycles. He tripped and fell on a spike on the hub of the back wheel. When he fell, the spike stabbed right into his eye. He screamed. Maybeth went dashing into the room to see blood pouring out of his eye. There was no missionary doctor anywhere near. Ken called the Chinese doctor who had some foreign training and he came over and examined Ian. By the time he arrived the eye was swollen to a large ball and was tightly shut. The doctor said that he couldn't tell anything until the swelling went down, but he poured some disinfectant into the tightly shut eye to prevent infection. Ken and Maybeth suffered a few anxious days as they prayed that the Lord would heal Ian's eye. Finally as the third day passed, they could see through a small slit that the eye seemed uninjured. What had been cut was the corner of the lid. Ian carried that little triangular shaped scar on his eyelid the rest of his life. Ken and Maybeth, so far from hospitals, were again so very thankful for the direct protection of God in that answer to prayer.

The daily routine of serving food and taking care of refugees was interrupted frequently by air raid alarms and many times the Japanese would be rumored to be approaching. Their friend, John Davis, nick-named John the Baptist, in a close-by mission station said he had been debating whether it was too dangerous to stay in this part of China. He joked that in Proverbs 28:1 he read that "The wicked flee when no man pursueth, but the righteous are as bold as a lion." But then Proverbs 29:1 read, "He that being often reproved and hardeneth his neck shall suddenly be cut off and that without remedy." "Now," he said, "the American consul keeps telling us that we should get out of this area. We have thought that we would leave, relying on Proverbs 29:1, but if you want to stay, you can stay, relying on Proverbs 28:1." Ken and Maybeth elected to stay for a while longer.

Once again, in the summer of 1944, the rumors of the approaching Japanese materialized into fact, and they had to leave the city of Chuhsien. They had known for some time that they would have to leave if the Japanese were indeed advancing on the city since Ian was only two and Maybeth was expecting another baby. Again, they left with Ken on his bicycle and Ian and Maybeth in a rickshaw along with a bit of baggage. The rickshaw man was not terribly strong and found it very difficult to pull and so Maybeth periodically got out and left Ian in the rickshaw with the baggage and walked alongside. They headed back to the province of Kiangsi. Maybeth, pregnant, weary and tired felt as though she walked most of the 20 miles or so. She dreaded the unsettled, uncertain life of a refugee again, but trusted that God was in control and would do what was best.

CHAPTER TWENTY-FIVE

They arrived at last at a mission station in Changshan, still in the province of Zhejiang, where a young couple had just settled down for their honeymoon-- sort of a honeymoon on the job. They were Canadians, Marvin and Miriam Dunn. The house there had been vacated by the previous missionaries and then occupied by Chinese refugees. It was simply filthy with discarded clothing items, left during the hot summer months in which the insects had multiplied beyond imagination. It had been shaken badly by the bombing of the city and had developed large cracks in all the plaster walls. Out of these cracks would come swarming bedbugs, fleas and other unidentifiable creatures. Miriam and Marvin came to this house still on cloud nine from their honeymoon and went to work cleaning up the house with the energy of the young.

No sooner had they cleaned it up than refugees like Ken and Maybeth began to drop in on them from mission stations in more dangerous parts of the country. Maybeth was so weary she could hardly put one foot in front of the other when she arrived at their house. She and Ken and little Ian received a warm welcome although the Dunns apologized for their lack of household furniture. Ken and Maybeth slept on the floor because there was no bed. Maybeth turned over the care of Ian to Ken and collapsed, happy to be off her feet. The only piece of furniture in the room was an apple box turned on end for them to use for shelves. They rigged mosquito nets, the most important piece of equipment for any travelers in China then. Mosquito nets were the only defense against malaria, a fever Ken and Maybeth and even Ian had all suffered often. Marvin and Miriam anxiously tried to round up enough food for the travelers they had so graciously welcomed. Ken and Maybeth were not the first visitors and certainly not the last as once again missionaries became

175

refugees and headed through their city on their way further south to Kanhsien in southern Kiangsi.

They were not there for more than a few days, before Miriam and Maybeth made plans for the arrival of the new baby. Miriam was a nurse trained in England. In fact, she was a gold medalist in obstetric nursing in her class in nursing school, and she promised Maybeth that she would follow her south to be with her when the baby came. Ken had helped with Ian's birth and had supreme confidence that he could take care of any emergency, however, the promise of a qualified nurse helped Maybeth breathe easier.

The Mission leaders thought that they should travel on from Changshan to Hokow, settle there and have the baby there. They arrived in Hokow, another 60 miles to the southwest, and found the mission station to be very old and very old fashioned. It was a two story wooden house with a long upstairs hallway with rooms on both sides and another long hallway downstairs with rooms on both sides. It was a very uninteresting looking house with a garden in the back, a mass of weeds that had grown head high and higher. The garden must have been pretty at one time, but no one had the time to take care of it, making it a complete wilderness.

A sweet single missionary, Miss McQueen, who waited on Maybeth hand and foot, occupied the house. She was quite particular about hygiene and because of that would not have a Chinese cook. It was customary to have Chinese servants, since they could be hired for about $5 a month which left the missionaries more time to do mission work. Five dollars a month was a high wage and was much better than a cook could get anywhere else. Perhaps because of her fear that a Chinese cook wouldn't practice strict enough hygiene, this dear little lady did all the cooking herself.

Of all places, this house was where Ian contracted dysentery. He was really very sick with it. He had come through so many filthy places unscathed that it was a bit embarrassing that he would get dysentery there in Hokow. Miss McQueen believed that one contracted dysentery by sitting on hot stones, not from any sort of contamination of food, and

Ken and Maybeth really couldn't say much about it all since they had made a practice of sitting on big slabs of stone which held the heat while the evening became cool.

Ian quickly recovered, however, and entertained them all with his latest delight: tools. He had a little hammer and delighted in finding pieces of wood that he could try to nail together. Miss McQueen was a tidy housekeeper and one day as Maybeth was going down the hall, she saw her pick up a little pile of pieces of wood and nails that Ian had left there when something more interesting had commanded his interest.

Maybeth stopped her and said, "Let me pick up after my own child. You certainly shouldn't have to do that!"

Her reply was, "Oh, but maybe it was me that left them there!" It certainly was a gracious attitude in her since it was ludicrous to think that she would leave a hammer and pieces of wood around.

Although she was gracious, Maybeth felt that she was a bit anxious about many things. This was the Gwansin River mission station, historically occupied only by single lady missionaries. In fact, Maybeth's mother had served as a missionary at this mission station before she was married. Suddenly Maybeth had descended upon her with Ken and a toddler and the baby coming and it all was a bit overwhelming for her. Soon, however, a few more missionaries arrived and then a missionary family, the John Birches.

It was August and sweltering hot. Mr. Birch took his children down to the Gwansin River to swim. The Gwansin River was an all-purpose river. The city would wash its clothes in the river, empty its chamber pots in the river, and draw water for tea out of the river.

One day one of the Birch children, Miriam, came back from swimming and that evening came down with a low-grade fever and said that she had trouble moving her legs. No one had any idea what could have been the trouble. As the days went by she had more trouble moving her legs. One of the older missionary ladies in the home, Miss McDonald, insisted on going to the child's room every day and massaging her legs thoroughly. No one knew if that was a good thing to do or not, but Miss McDonald was convinced that it was what she needed to do. Every day she would massage the child's legs very thoroughly. Even with the massaging, Miriam soon was unable to use her legs for walking and resorted to crawling where she needed to go. When the Birches, months later, reached medical help, they discovered that Miriam had contracted polio, a disease no one had really heard much about at the time. The doctors who treated her said that the treatment she had received at the hand of Miss McDonald was the very best treatment they would have suggested at the time had they been there. Again God provided for His children in perilous times.

Ian found a little turtle and immediately adopted it for a pet. He kept it in their room, played with it and found food for it. Miss McQueen had a paralyzing horror of turtles and often stated that she did not want to see any turtles around her. Her room was at the opposite end of the hall from theirs, but she made her fears known very clearly to both Ken and Maybeth. One day they lost Ian's little turtle; they hunted everywhere to no avail. Of course, it eventually turned up in Miss McQueen's wastebasket. She was very annoyed, but managed to hide it well.

One hot day in September, word reached the group in Hokow that the Japanese had almost completely encircled Kiangsi province and that no one should stay any longer in Hokow. The American consul informed the missionaries that the Japanese were on the north and the south and that their only chance to escape was to flee to the American airbase in Kanhsien, where Ian had been born. From there in the south of the Kiangsi province, they could fly an American plane to Kunming, another American airbase and perhaps get evacuated to west China. Ken and Maybeth did not hold out any hope of getting out of China at that time even though their first term in China had been nine years, much longer than any missionary ever expected to stay without a furlough in the homeland. They were told that they could waste no time since the airbase was preparing to close, leaving only the personnel to fly out themselves.

How could Ken and Maybeth possibly move? Ian was almost two and the baby was due almost any day. They stayed and watched daily as their fellow missionaries moved down to the airbase and safety. Soon they found themselves almost alone on the mission station with Miriam Dunn, the maternity nurse, who had come down from Changshan to help deliver the baby and one other single missionary, Winnie Rand. Their fears of being captured by the Japanese became more intense each day, and yet they didn't want to move and risk the baby coming while they were on the road without any shelter or help.

Finally, on September 27, 1944, Maybeth started at the top of the enormous two-story house and scrubbed the floors. They were wood floors, rough with splinters occasionally, and very dirty. She scrubbed all the floors in the house and at the end of the day was really exhausted. Her attempts to bring on labor worked. That night she had her first labor pains and Ken and Winnie and Miriam all worked together to help bring Wendy, a beautiful, healthy baby girl, into the world on the kitchen table in the mission station. Ken and Maybeth were so thankful that she had finally arrived safely, and determined that at the earliest possible chance they were going to head down south to the airbase in Kanhsien.

CHAPTER TWENTY-SIX

Sometime in that first week, Miriam and Winnie left, leaving the Gray family alone in the big, rambling mission station. They knew that time was of the essence since the Japanese had continued to advance. Rumors flew around the city and they prayed for deliverance daily. When Wendy was about ten days old, Ken and Maybeth decided that it was time to go. They gathered the children up, filled a very small bag with whatever luggage they deemed essential, (mostly diapers) and took a train to Kienchangfu. They really had very few belongings and it made no sense to take much since by that time they hoped that they would be out of China before too long. They were headed for Kanhsien almost 300 miles away, not knowing how they would manage to get there and not knowing if they could stay ahead of the Japanese army. The train was terribly slow; Maybeth kept thinking that they could have walked faster than it went. That night they stayed in a little inn. In the room was an old dresser, and having no other bed for the baby, they pulled out one of the drawers and put the baby in the drawer for a bed. She really didn't have much of a bed at all until she was much older.

The following day when Ken was outside in the city, he met a British military officer, a young fellow in his early twenties who had been trained in commando warfare. This young man had a military truck and he told Ken that he was leaving the next morning to go to Kanhsien. Anytime a vehicle left a city in those days, the Chinese refugees were quick to try to scramble on and ride along, and Ken knew that most military truck drivers had strict orders to take no passengers. Ken put aside his natural inclination to be polite and asked this young man if he and his little family could ride in the truck. To his amazement, the officer quickly assented. He said he would not be taking anyone else, but, Ken's family was very welcome to come along. Ken and Maybeth again saw the hand of God in their escape. The next morning saw them climbing aboard a big truck. The young officer drove and he helped Maybeth and the baby up in the front with him and told Ken that he and Ian would have to sit in the open back of the truck.

They traveled this way for several days. As they went south the days grew hotter and their progress was agonizingly slow on poor roads with detours on even dustier roads. Ken contracted a very bad eye infection, becoming more painful as time passed. Maybeth sat at the front with Wendy and whenever the baby would stir and make small noises, Maybeth would throw a blanket over her shoulder and nurse her discreetly under the blanket. The baby was very content since she had milk on demand and so never cried at all. At the end of the first day, this young officer, who apparently was too young to know better, said, "That baby is amazing. She never cried all day and she never ate a thing."

That night they stayed in an inn with the baby back in a dresser drawer. Maybeth began to be concerned about running out of clean diapers and how to clean the dirty ones and their dirty clothes. She knew that there was no way to know when she would be able to wash anything. She felt dirty and could do nothing about it and worse yet, her supply of diapers was quickly running out. The second night the young officer asked her if they would mind staying in a Roman Catholic compound since he knew of some Catholic sisters who worked in that city. He assured Ken and Maybeth that they would be very glad to put them up. Maybeth was delighted and hoped she would find water and soap and be able to clean up and wash diapers.

They arrived at about 11:00 p.m. and, although the sisters were not expecting them, they welcomed the family, took them into their compound immediately. They gave them a hot meal and then showed them to a clean little room with a bed with clean sheets. What a luxury that felt! Again they pulled out the dresser drawer and wrapped Wendy up and put her in it. Ian had a little cot to sleep on and after that good meal they settled down to sleep.

Before they slept, Maybeth gathered her dirty clothes and started to wash them in the basin in the room, a monumental task as she looked at all the dirty clothes and diapers of several days hard traveling. How would she get enough water to wash them all and how could she get them dry? In immediate answer to her unspoken cry, a soft-spoken Canadian sister came to her door, knocked, and said, "If you have a baby and a little boy, you've got dirty clothes. Let me have your diapers and your baby's clothes and I'll wash them for you and be sure to have them dry by the morning when you have to leave."

Maybeth told her that they had to leave by early morning, about 6 a.m., but she insisted and took her bundle of dirty things.

They went to bed and slept well, short though the night was. It was so refreshing to sleep in a clean place with clean sheets and protection. The sisters had made them so welcome and exhibited such godliness that they were overwhelmed.

The next morning they were awakened and fed hot pancakes which they all thoroughly enjoyed, Ian especially, and then the same sister came in with a stack of clean and folded diapers and clothes. The diapers were washed and bleached, spotless and ironed. She had no washing machine or dryer since there was no electricity and yet she had washed all those things out by hand and then ironed them. She would have washed the diapers on a scrub board one by one and then dried them over a charcoal fire and then ironed them with a charcoal iron. Maybeth looked at her and said, "How can I ever thank you? You've been up all night doing this, haven't you?"

She said, "Yes, but that's all right; I was glad to do it."

"But I have no way to repay you for all this."

And she said, "As I did these diapers, I thought of what our Lord had said, 'Inasmuch as ye have done it unto one of the least of these my brethren, ye have done it unto me.' I did it for His sake."

Maybeth's eyes filled with tears as she looked into the face of another one of God's children that she had met at the most unexpected place, doing tasks for her for His sake. God's words were that "A cup of cold water given in my name will have its reward" and Maybeth was confident that this dear saint received her reward. Those sisters never left China throughout the upheaval and ensuing Communist takeover and Maybeth never heard what happened to them.

The third day's driving brought them to the American airbase in Kanhsien, Soon after their arrival one of the airmen ran up to Maybeth and asked if that was a baby she had in her arms.

"Yes," she said.

"How old is the baby?" he asked.

"She is about two weeks old," Maybeth replied.

"Oh," he said. "Let me see. I just got word that my wife has had a baby and she would be about two weeks old. Let me see what they look like at that age." He was so delighted to hold the little baby and imagine that it was his own child whom he would not be seeing for a long time yet.

The airmen crowded around Ian and Wendy then since it had been a long time since they had seen a white child and many had children at home. One of them gave Ian a chocolate bar and never having seen one before, he didn't quite know what to do with it. The pretty colored paper fascinated him, so he let the chocolate drop and kept the paper. He didn't like the ice cream another tried to give him. He thought it was too cold. The same reaction happened when they gave him a banana. He didn't know what to do with it. He had never seen a chocolate bar before or ice cream or a banana. It was a whole new world of food. The family had their dinner there at the airbase and Maybeth couldn't get over the abundance of food. In fact, she was astonished at all the food that was wasted after she and Ken had scrounged for food for so long, never really having enough. They were thin and wasted after having been so short of food for so many years and it was a strange experience for them to see so much food wasted on each plate as the airmen filled up and pushed the remainder in the garbage.

They boarded the next-to-last plane to ferry missionaries out to west China before the airbase closed. The plane was a troop plane with bucket seats along the sides. It was certainly not terribly comfortable, but the pilot came and talked to Maybeth before they departed the airbase. He said, " We fly very high to avoid Japanese anti-aircraft fire, but you watch that baby very closely and if the tips of her ears or the tip of her nose begins to look a little blue, you tell me and we'll go lower and brave the anti-aircraft." Maybeth was so touched that he would do that. As they flew she watched the baby carefully, but Wendy weathered that trip just fine with no ill effects.

They flew into Kunming that night and there they were met by their dear friends, Bill and Vera Tyler, who were in charge of the mission station there. They too had moved because of the Japanese advance and were hosting the many missionaries who were getting out of China. How good it was to see them again after the year they had spent together. Every room in every house belonging to the Mission was jammed full of fleeing missionaries and their families. When Ken and Maybeth arrived, they were given one room for the four of them.

Ken's eye infection had not improved and was terribly painful. He was able to contact the medical personnel there at the airbase and the medic in charge examined his eye. Although there had not been a release of the drug known as sulfa, this man had a small supply of it and gave some to Ken. In about a week it cleared up all the infection in Ken's eye. What a wonderful gift that was!

The morning after they arrived in Kunming, Ken, Maybeth and Ian, in their weakened state came down with malaria. They all felt weak and feverish and each morning Ken and Maybeth would reach for the thermometer; the one who had the lower temperature had to get up and look after the family. So if Ken's temperature was 103 degrees and Maybeth's was 104, he would have to get up, change the baby, take care of Ian and do the chores for all of them. After that he would get back into bed again. They still found ways to have fun over being that sick! They debated whether it was worse to have the higher temperature or the lower.

They received word a few days later that the last plane full of missionaries that flew out of Kanhsien had crashed on the mountains and that all the passengers had been killed. A dearly loved senior missionary, Graham Hutchinson and his wife died on the flight, and they grieved for his family and for their own loss. They had meant so much to Ken and

Maybeth and had insisted that they would send everyone else ahead and be the last ones to leave Kanhsien. Later in Ken and Maybeth's lives they named a son Graham because of their love for Mr Hutchinson.

Bill and Vera Tyler were good to Ken and Maybeth in their illness and need of rest. They spent a much needed few weeks there in Kunming to rest up before continuing on with their journey. It was certain that they were going to leave China for home then, and they made arrangements to fly out of Kunming via public airline into Calcutta, India.

Kunming was high in the mountains and the family had brought winter clothes. Ken had a wool suit that he wore everywhere. It was, in fact, his wedding suit, but he had hardly any shirt left. Maybeth had mended the one white shirt he had until there was nothing left but the collar and a strip down the front. First, she had turned the collar when it began to fray. Then she had taken pieces of the back to mend the sleeves. Then when the elbows wore out, she had taken pieces of the sleeves to mend the front, until there was barely anything left of the shirt. A casual observer might not have noticed anything, though, because the starched white collar was still visible and the strip down the front usually stayed in place and gave the appearance of a full shirt. There were no cuffs of course, but few noticed that. Goods were so scarce in the war time years in China that there was no way they could have found a white shirt like that. They had sold many of their belongings, finding that the prices they received were many times greater than they had paid for those same items nine years earlier. They sold an old typewriter for ten times what they had paid for it because of the shortages. A newspaper reporter paid them much more than they would have even asked. With their clothing mostly sold, all they had were the winter clothes they had expected to need for the cold weather there in Kunming.

As they left China and boarded the plane for India, Maybeth wore a winter coat and Ken wore his woolen suit. The flight over the Hump, as the Himalayan Mountains were termed, was a new experience. The flight took them over Burma and down into India. Maybeth got terribly airsick. Her natural motion sickness was exaggerated because the plane would fly over high mountains and the view would be close to the peak and then the canyons would drop away quickly on the other side of the mountain and she could see all the way down to the river, looking like a little strip of ribbon winding through the canyons. Then they would cross a peak where she could see little huts high up on the mountain and the land would rise up to meet her eyes and then would drop away on the other side. It certainly was spectacular, but Maybeth's motion sickness ruined her enjoyment of the trip considerably.

CHAPTER TWENTY-SEVEN

When they landed in Calcutta, they had been instructed to go to a certain mission station where the CIM had written ahead to confirm accommodations for them. They arrived in a city, consumed by a burning hot sun. There they were on the hot airport runway in winter clothing, and the heat was overwhelming. They managed to get a taxi to take them to the appointed mission station. When they arrived, they discovered that the people in charge of the mission house had not received any message that they were coming and had no place for them to stay.

Maybeth's weariness and discouragement caught up with her as she and Ken and the children stood outside the home and were told that there was simply no room. They were hot, tired, the children were uncomfortable, and they had had a terrifying nine years. It seemed to be too much that there was no room when they eventually reached safety. Maybeth sat on the steps of that house in the heat with Wendy in her arms and Ian sitting beside her as Ken went looking for some place for them to stay. The weeks and years of tension, sickness, fear, and weariness came rushing over her and she cried and cried. Little Ian cuddled up to her in an attempt to comfort her. Here they were with the wrong kind of clothes on, with no place to stay, little money, tired to the bone, and in this unknown world of India. On top of that it was Calcutta which looked to be the most poverty-stricken, pathetic place in the world she had ever been.

An hour later, Ken reemerged from the house with another missionary and said that they had found a place across the park where the people in the house had said they could have a room. There was a park right there in the front of the mission house and this place was on the other side of this small park. They would have to come across the park for meals at the mission home. At this point they were glad of any place to rest.

One of their first tasks was to go out into the city to buy a shirt for Ken so that he could take off his suit coat. It was terribly hot, but if he had taken off his coat, he'd have had nothing on underneath except a collar and a strip down the front!

The next day, Sunday, the family went to a little Anglican church and wept all the way through the service. They certainly drew some stares, but it was so good to sing familiar hymns in English and worship God in their native language! They were moved by the service and by God's marvelous protection of them in the years past. As they began to sing the hymns, the tears streamed down their faces as they marveled at how good it was to sing hymns and hear a sermon in English among people who already felt like old friends simply because they spoke English.

The room was adequate. There was a little wicker bed for Wendy and a small camp cot for Ian. The arrangement was fine with Maybeth, until she learned that the mission station was glad to provide them with their meals, but didn't want them to bring the baby over with them for meals, apparently for fear that her crying might disturb the meal. Safety was not an issue, but the only thing they could think to do was to time her feedings so that she would be asleep while they walked the short distance across the park to the mission home for meals and after hur-riedly eating, rush back. Maybeth hated to leave her even though she slept solidly usually for several hours. Why it was that the folk in this mission station didn't want them to bring her seemed a mystery. Ian was welcome, but not the baby. One time she had apparently awakened not long after Maybeth left and had cried the whole time she was gone rubbing her little head on the wicker of the cot until her forehead was red. Maybeth felt just sick and she and Ken were very uncomfortable with the arrangement.

It was a relief, then, when a few days later the CIM contacted them with the suggestion that they move to Bombay, on the other side of India to get away from the crowded conditions there in Calcutta. They gladly agreed and arranged to take the train. Travel on Indian trains was an experience they would not forget. The trains were jammed with people. Maybeth was fortunate to have a seat at all. Ken stood some of the time and shared a seat with Maybeth some of the time, both with children on their laps. They all had to sit straight up with no room to even wiggle. Both children were very good, but it wasn't easy for them. The mass of humanity made for loud, smelly, hot, sticky conditions.

Arriving in Bombay, imagine their delight to find waiting for them at the train station, the Sharmans. They had arrived earlier and it was so good to see them. They still held a special spot in both Maybeth's and Ken's hearts because of their understanding comfort when Gwen had died. They hadn't seen them since that time, six years before, and they cherished the time to be together. They had two little boys and Maybeth and Ken had their two. They stayed in the same house with Jack and Peggy for a week or two singing, sharing stories and enjoying one another's company. Then they moved to another part of Bombay, to a lovely big home owned by the American Methodist Missionary Society.

Ken and Maybeth were given a beautiful apartment with Persian rugs on the floor and furnished with fashionable and comfortable chairs and furniture. The missionaries in charge, Mr. and Mrs. Aldis, made them comfortable at once. They stayed in that lovely home for eight or nine months.

The Aldises did so much for them and for all the refugees from China during those days. At that time there were six couples with seven children from the China Inland Mission pushing their hospitality to the breaking point as well as several of their own American Methodist missionaries waiting to sail home. Mrs. Aldis acted as if it were a privilege to manage the households and help with meals. She was so gracious and the food was perhaps the best they'd had since early days in China before the war began. Maybeth, and especially Ken, needed good food after many years of short rations. They were both too thin and suffered from malaria frequently. Their systems needed good nutrition and rest and their hearts needed consolation after the previous nine years. They had a big room right next to the dining room for easy access and the

Aldis couple seemed to take a special interest in them and their children. It was just before the monsoon season and the heat outdoors was almost unbearable, but the big old stone house was cool.

Ken was told that it would be a long time before they could book passage for home. The war was still going, and the British and American ships were fearful of being torpedoed on the long haul across the Atlantic, and as a result would not allow any children under the age of six to travel to America on them. Presumably life jackets would not fit children under the age of six, so Ken and Maybeth knew they would have a long wait until circumstances changed or the war ended. With a baby a month old, they entertained no idea of leaving anytime soon. Once they understood the state of travel, they determined that they would take what God had provided and rest and enjoy India. Ken gained about 20 pounds and Maybeth gained some too. They felt strong and healthy again. They attended a little church that had services in English led by a young Anglo-Indian. They came to love him and the fellowship of that church.

Bombay was a beautiful city. Down the main streets were gorgeous Flame-of-the-Forest trees and just before the monsoon season they were filled with masses of blooms, red-orange flowers. Meals were regular and nutritious, and Ken enjoyed Indian food with its characteristic flavors and methods of preparation. Travel could be accomplished by the garry, a vehicle with two seats and a driver, the garrywalla, sitting high up ahead driving the horse, or donkey. Sometimes they would go to the movies also. Maybeth always remembered seeing one beautiful movie called "A Song to Remember", the story of the life and love of the composer, Frederic Chopin. It was romantic and fun, and after nine and a half years of war and bombing and heartbreak and hunger, it was good to find themselves safe in that peaceful city and surrounded by so many people they loved.

While friends and other missionaries came and went home on furlough, Ken and Maybeth remained. They were on the waiting list for the American Express, waiting to get out of India, but always being passed up because their children were too small.

While visiting an American couple in the north of India, Maybeth developed a high fever and she and Ken decided that it was unfair for this missionary family to take care of sick people when their work demanded much of their time. They traveled back to Bombay and Maybeth went straight to bed. The doctor diagnosed infectious hepatitis and insisted that she go immediately by ambulance to the hospital. Maybeth objected that she was nursing a baby, but the doctor was unyielding and insisted that Ken would simply have to wean the baby. She was taken to the British hospital, leaving Ken to take care of two-year-old Ian and the baby, Wendy. He had to buy baby bottles and work out a sort of formula. Ken always proudly claimed that he weaned Wendy. He had no babysitting arrangement, however, and so found it difficult to go to the hospital on the other side of Bombay to visit Maybeth.

The British hospital, although administered by the British, was run by Indian nurses and orderlies. The treatment for hepatitis was apparently to drink vast quantities of fluids. Maybeth would be given a pitcher of water with limejuice in it and told to have it finished by noon. Then she was given the same treatment in the afternoon. She was placed in a public ward with twenty beds in the room.

Maybeth was the only white patient and she discovered after talking with the head nurse, who spoke English, that the other side of the room was filled with typhoid patients. Those patients were under orders to eat only what the hospital prepared for them, but their relatives would come to visit and bring them other food which they would eat with delight, hiding it under their pillow when the doctor or nurse approached. At night, when they were supposed to leave, the same relatives would hide under the bed and sleep there all night. On Maybeth's side of the room there were all kinds of diseases and nationalities, mostly Indian and Burmese.

Nurses akin to what might be called practical nurses, called ayahs, did most of the work in the ward. Most were very fat and chewed beetle nut, with the blood-red juice dripping out the sides of their mouths. They would wipe their chins with the back of their hand and then wipe their hands down the patients' bedspreads. Thus the bedspreads had red smears all over them, which eventually turned brown.

Maybeth was revolted, but gradually became resigned to the way medicine was practiced there. The head nurse, a British woman, was especially kind to Maybeth and suggested that when she was able to get out of bed, she could come and sit in her nurse's station. Maybeth's comment about the hospital stay was that "it was rough", undoubtedly a huge understatement. But, as she would add, "In spite of it all, I got better" and after ten days in the hospital, she was dismissed.

Her dismissal wasn't a result of her being cured. She was certainly not well enough to go home. During her ten days in the hospital, the Allies dropped on August 6 and August 9, two atomic bombs on Japan, an event that shook the world. The war was officially over on September 2, 1945, when Japan formally surrendered and she and Ken and the children would be able to return home, really home. Suddenly the nine and a half years in China and now in India seemed like a very long time. Going home lifted her spirits so greatly that the doctor dismissed her and she went home to Ken and the children to prepare for the trip home.

Ken meanwhile had been busy preparing and packing. He had been to the American Express office in Bombay and had been told that Sweden was sending a "nursing ship" to Bombay to transport the huge backup of Europeans and Americans who had been trapped there by the war. The ship was the "Gripsholm" and was scheduled to arrive in Bombay in a few days. Packing up took little time and there was plenty of time to enjoy being together again and to anticipate with huge excitement the trip home. Letters were written to parents and friends with the joyful news. Their hearts were bursting with joy as they thought of home and family waiting for them after such a long time.

Maybeth tried to force herself to rest now and then, but never had been good at that trick. She worked feverishly packing and taking care of the children as Ken went down to the docks to make arrangements for boarding the ship. He came home with the news that the Gripsholm was charging one flat rate for everyone on the ship no matter what class of room was available. So those in first class and those in steerage would pay the same reasonable rate. The ship's company had also decided that they would board people in the order of their name on the American

Express waiting list. It was customary in those days to sign on with an American Express office if you wanted transportation to America, and Ken had done that when he and Maybeth had arrived in Bombay. Ken and Maybeth had waited the longest in Bombay, close to a year, and their name was at the top of the list. Those who had been ahead of them on the list had shipped out already. Some had children who were older and some had no children, so Ken and Maybeth topped the list. Assignment of cabins was to be done according to the longest time people had waited in Bombay, and families with little children would have the best, and obviously largest, cabins.

On the day that the ship was scheduled to depart, Ken and Maybeth made their way down to the dock with their luggage and two small children in tow. To their amazement and delight, they discovered that they would be assigned the state cabin, one used by state department officials and heads of states. The cabin was more beautiful than any they had ever seen on shipboard before. It boasted a true double bed for Ken and Maybeth, a cot for Ian, and a crib for Wendy. The cabin had a mirror-lined bathroom attached to be used only by them. What luxury! The cabin was air-conditioned with every luxury they had forgotten about while living in desperate conditions in China for almost ten years. A Swedish nurse came to the cabin and introduced herself as their attendant. Other travelers on the ship came by and looked enviously at the cabin. One wealthy businessman traveling on the ship came by and angrily asked Ken if he had pull with the owners or if he had bribed someone to get a cabin like that. This businessman had paid the same price for passage and had a room on E deck while these poor people with the two small children had the best room on A deck. Ken patiently explained the process the American Express had used in assigning cabins.

The trip home was smooth and Maybeth didn't even feel seasick very much. The cabin was so comfortable and the food was excellent. Although the weather was incredibly hot through the Red Sea and the Suez Canal, they could retire to their air-conditioned cabin and relax. The Suez Canal fascinated them with the locks and the desert surrounding them. Ian saw his first sight of camels as the ship traveled up the Red Sea. They stopped at Port Said, north of Egypt, where vendors of all shapes and sizes scrambled aboard and sold leather goods and desert souvenirs.

From there they sailed to a poor little port in Greece, Piraeus. Ken and Maybeth were shocked to see how much Greece had suffered in the war. Their hearts went out to these poverty-stricken people. Small boys in boats approached the ship and sold sponges. They had spent the day before diving for them and were trying to make a little money selling their haul. Off in the distance Ken and Maybeth could make out the Acropolis and pondered the Biblical account of Paul, the Apostle, who traveled as a missionary there and spoke to the men of Athens about their statue to the unknown god. Paul brought news of God to those interested listeners as Ken and Maybeth had spent the last nine years doing. From there they sailed through the Mediterranean Sea, past Gibraltar, and out to sea headed for New York.

What a trip it was in such sublime luxury! Maybeth felt unworthy to be so blessed with such care and love after so many difficult years. When the Statue of Liberty came into view the tears streamed down their faces. The Gripsholm was arriving at the same time as many of the troop ships with men coming home from the war. Welcome ships came out to meet each troop ship with dancing and bands playing and huge "Welcome" signs flying. Although their ship did not have troops on board, they were given the same welcome and their hearts filled with joy. To be home again after such a long time and so many years, when they were never sure they would be home at all, was hard to believe. After seeing the cruelties of war and the effect of war on people and countries, the United States reached out sheltering arms for them, and they gladly entered the port of New York and home.

Looking back on that first term, filled with terror and sorrow as well as good times and love, as an old woman reminding her children, Maybeth was able to say,

God brought us through difficult situations, but when I look back now, I always think of God's faithfulness- faithfulness day by day, supplying our need. Sometimes Chinese Christians, taking pity on our need to travel so much, would empty their pockets and give to us. To be helped by the people whom we had come to help so touched our hearts. We would often stop and have prayer with Chinese Christians as we fled. We'd look them up or stop in churches along the way. Wherever we were, there were opportunities to witness, and our witness was of God's faithfulness, his love and his care.

We realized when we came home later that friends of ours had been praying for us and for all missionaries. Some who had promised to pray for us when we left said to us, "Oh, are you a missionary in China? We thought you were in India."' Many dropped their prayers as we dropped out of the scene and there was no news of us when letters didn't get through. But there were some who were so faithful! How we thanked God for those who tried to keep in touch with us. Sometimes it was almost impossible. But there were those who at least continually prayed for us, holding us up before God, with no knowledge of our conditions. We were so moved by the faithfulness and care of a loving God. We felt we were being held in the hollow of His hand, that He knew where we were, that we were never beyond His care, that we were never beyond His love. The friendship of other Christians of all nationalities was beautiful, regardless of denomination. The fact that we could pray together and commit our ways to the Lord together and feel concern for one another was such a blessing for each of us.

I feel that we saw so little lasting work in China; such as building up a church or watching one grow at that time. The second term we did more of that, but the first term was so much on the run. What we did learn was the love and care of God on a daily basis and we came to realize His love and care in a way that we never would have if we'd been in one place. I'm so glad that God called us out at a time like that; not for anything that we could do, but to show His faithfulness and His love whatever the conditions were. He had so many things to teach us and to prove His faithfulness."

Epilogue

Sixty-one years later Maybeth's daughter, this writer, returned to China in the company of the daughter of Jack and Peggy Sharman and visited the cities of Fenghua, Ninghai, Linhai, Chenghsien (now Shengzhou) and Tientai, following the route of Maybeth and Ken Gray in their flight from the Japanese Army.

Everywhere we went we were greeted lovingly by members of the church who had survived the Cultural Revolution and grown in their faith. Arriving in Tientai, however, was a particularly heart-rending moment, since it was in Tientai that my older sister, Gwen, had died so many years ago. We visited the house where Gwen had lived for a day or two before she died. The tears came easily. The kind people of the church were anxious to know the story of the little girl who had died a refugee in their city.

The following day a national "elder day" celebration was held in the church and we sat down to a marvelous lunch of noodles and shrimp in the courtyard of the old building. We were surrounded by the elderly, people who were old enough to remember our parents, and although the language barrier prevented extensive conversation, the love shone in their eyes. One dear lady kept picking the shrimp out of her noodles and putting them in mine. Meat was especially precious and she was giving her meat to me.

At the program to honor the elderly, a bouquet was presented to me from the members of the church in honor of Gwen. It was an armful of roses and lilies. Roses and lilies had been placed on Gwen's grave when she was buried in Linhai. It was as though they were recalling the refusal of their town fathers to offer a place of burial for a little child back in 1942. It was a demonstration of the compassion that had been missing then.

The name, Tientai, means "platform to heaven" and the city is located in beautiful mountainous surroundings. Waterfalls plunge down steep cliffs to the west of the city and the mountains rise behind it. In many ways, Tientai was a welcoming city in 2006 and little Gwen who surrendered her life there in 1942 had indeed found it a platform to heaven.

The love shown by the church in Tientai validated the suffering that my mother had experienced there. God had turned her grief into blessing for His church in China.

ABOUT THE AUTHOR

Born in Shanghai, China, the child of third generation missionaries, Esther and her family were driven out of China in 1950 and spent several years on a farm in Canada before moving to the United States in 1957. As a teenager she became a naturalized U.S. citizen.

She attended Geneva College in western Pennsylvania and graduated with a B.A. in English in 1968. Following graduation she married and began a teaching career that spanned thirty years.

A love of adventure sent Esther and her husband, Alex, to Wyoming in 1970 where they settled and raised a family. They quickly grew to love the wide open spaces and take yearly horse pack trips to the mountains and wilderness areas of Wyoming.